Brilliant computing for the Over 50s

P.K. MacBride

PEARSON
Prentice
Hall

Harlow, England • London • New York • Boston • San Francisco • Toronto • Sydney • Singapore • Hong Kong
Tokyo • Seoul • Taipei • New Delhi • Cape Town • Madrid • Mexico City • Amsterdam • Munich • Paris • Milan

Pearson Education Limited
Edinburgh Gate
Harlow
Essex CM20 2JE
England

and Associated Companies throughout the world

Visit us on the World Wide Web at:
www.pearsoned.co.uk

First published 2006

ISBN-13: 978-0-13-188812-8
ISBN-10: 0-13-188812-9

British Library Cataloguing-in-Publication Data
A catalogue record for this book is available from the British Library

Library of Congress Cataloging-in-Publication Data
A catalog record for this book is available from the Library of Congress

10 9 8 7 6 5 4 3 2 1
10 09 08 07 06

Prepared for Pearson Education Ltd by Syllaba Ltd (http://www.syllaba.co.uk).
Typeset in 12pt Arial Condensed by 30
Printed and bound in Great Britain by Ashford Colour Press Ltd., Gosport.

The publisher's policy is to use paper manufactured from sustainable forests.

Brilliant guides

What you need to know and how to do it

When you come up against a problem that you're unsure how to solve, or want to accomplish something that you aren't sure how to do, where do you look? Manuals and traditional training guides are usually too big and unwieldy and are intended to be used as end-to-end training resources, making it hard to get to the info you need right away without having to wade through pages of background information that you just don't need at that moment – and helplines are rarely that helpful!

Brilliant guides have been developed to allow you to find the info you need easily and without fuss and guide you through the task using a highly visual, step-by-step approach – providing exactly what you need to know when you need it!

Brilliant guides provide the quick easy-to-access information that you need, using a table of contents and troubleshooting guide to help you find exactly what you need to know, and then presenting each task in a visual manner. Numbered steps guide you through each task or problem, using numerous screenshots to illustrate each step. Added features include 'See also' boxes that point you to related tasks and information in the book, while 'Did you know?' sections alert you to relevant expert tips, tricks and advice to further expand your skills and knowledge.

In addition to covering all major office PC applications, and related computing subjects, the *Brilliant* series also contains titles that will help you in every aspect of your working life, such as writing the perfect CV, answering the toughest interview questions and moving on in your career.

Brilliant guides are the light at the end of the tunnel when you are faced with any minor or major task.

Publisher's acknowledgements

The author and publisher would like to thank the web masters of the following sites for permission to reproduce the screen shots in this book:

Yahoo! UK, Google UK, Saga, Real and Yamaha Motor Co.

Microsoft product screen shots reprinted with permission from Microsoft Corporation. FujiFilm screen shots reprinted with permission from FujiFilm Electronic Imaging Ltd.

Every effort has been made to obtain necessary permission with reference to copyright material. In some instances we have been unable to trace the owners of copyright material, and we would appreciate any information that would enable us to do so.

Author's acknowledgements

The author would like to thank Karen, Sally and Andy for making this project so enjoyable.

About the author

P.K. MacBride spent 20 years at the chalkface in schools and technical colleges before leaving to work full-time as a writer, editor and typesetter. He has written over 100 books, mainly on computing topics, covering many aspects of computer programming, software applications and the internet. He has been translated into over a dozen languages, including Russian, Portugese, Greek, Chinese and American.

Contents

Preface

The basic unit of computer memory is called a byte, but computers don't bite. And you can't do much damage to them either, whatever you do wrong – short of taking a hammer to them. The worst that can normally happen is that it will stop working, half-way through a job and that's easily solved – just turn it off and on again. For the most part, computer systems are logical, work in standard ways and follow the same set of basic rules. Once you understand those rules, you will be able to use your computer effectively, and tackle new applications confidently. This book will show you those rules. So, shed your fears. You can't break it, and it won't break you.

Being over 50 is no handicap when it comes to learning about computers. I'm over 50, though I've been using computers for 20-odd years, but I have many friends and relations who have come to computers, and mastered them, in their 50s, 60s, 70s and even 80s. We can all learn new things at any age. The biggest bar to learning is the belief that it will be difficult. Relax, using a computer is not difficult. (Designing a computer or developing new computer applications are, but no-one is asking you to do these things!)

Being over 50 may well, however, affect the sort of things that you want to learn about computers. If I had been writing this book for the under 50s, I would have included chapters on the full range of office applications: word processing, spreadsheets, databases and presentation software, because younger people may well need these to take their careers forward. Us older folks, if we are still in work, probably have all the IT skills we need for the job, and if we are now starting to learn about computers, it is for use in our leisure activities. We want to use them to write letters, minutes of meetings or our memoirs; create newsletters and posters for our clubs, store, edit, organise and print our digital photos and videos; get online and explore the internet. And that's what this book is about.

There are several different types of computer around, and lots of software. This book is for people who have a PC (of any make), running Windows XP, with either Word or Works as your word processor. I've assumed that if you have a digital camera, you will have Photoshop (or something very similar). Apart from that, all the software that is covered in this book is supplied as part of the Windows XP package – and that is all most of us need.

P.K. MacBride, Southampton 2006

Introduction

Welcome to *Brilliant Computing for the Over 50s*, a visual quick reference book that shows you how to make the most of your PC. Focused specifically on the needs of those whose working life was not affected significantly by computers, it provides an introductory guide to using a computer. It will show you how to work in the Windows environment, organise your files, use a word processor, store and edit images from a camera, configure Windows to suit you, and will start you off exploring the internet and communicating by email.

Find what you need to know – when you need it

You don't have to read this book in any particular order. We've designed the book so that you can jump in, get the information you need, and jump out. To find the information that you need, just look up the task in the table of contents or Troubleshooting guide, and turn to the page listed. Read the task introduction, follow the step-by-step instructions along with the illustration, and you're done.

How this book works

Each task is presented with step-by-step instructions in one column and screen illustrations in the other. This arrangement lets you focus on a single task without having to turn the pages too often.

Step-by-step instructions

This book provides concise step-by-step instructions that show you how to accomplish a task. Each set of instructions includes illustrations that directly correspond to the easy-to-read steps. Eye-catching text features provide additional helpful information in bite-sized chunks to help you work more efficiently or to teach you more in-depth information. The 'For your information' feature provides tips and techniques to help you work smarter, while the 'See also' cross-references lead you to other parts of the book containing related information about the task. Essential information is highlighted in 'Important' boxes that will ensure you don't miss any vital suggestions and advice.

Troubleshooting guide

This book offers quick and easy ways to diagnose and solve common problems that you might encounter using the Troubleshooting guide. The problems are grouped into categories that are presented alphabetically.

Spelling

We have used UK spelling conventions throughout this book. You may therefore notice some inconsistencies between the text and the software on your computer which is likely to have been developed in the USA. We have however adopted US spelling for the words 'disk' and 'program' as these are becoming commonly accepted throughout the world.

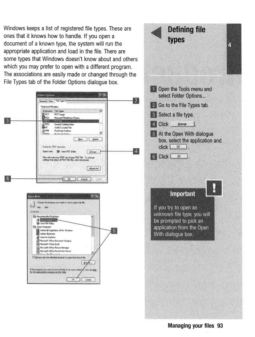

Managing your files 93

Troubleshooting guide

Instant computing

Introduction

Computing does not have to be difficult. You don't need a degree in Computer Science to produce a letter or the minutes of a meeting with a word processor, or to draw a picture or diagram on the screen. (Of course, you do need a degree in Computer Science, or something like it, if you are going to develop new software or design new equipment, but that's not what we're about here!) In this first chapter you will see how little you need to learn to be able to do useful things with your computer. We will explore three applications that are present in every Windows XP computer:

- WordPad, a simple but effective word processor
- My Computer, which is used for managing files
- Paint, a basic application for creating and editing images.

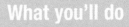

Important

Windows XP allows its users to customise the screen in many ways. As a result, your screen may well not look exactly the same as the ones in the screenshots. You will see how to customise the display in Chapter 7.

Discovering your PC

A desktop PC system typically has these components:

Monitor or VDU (Visual Display Unit). On most desktop PCs this is similar to a TV, though flat LCD screens are becoming more common. Newer monitors usually have 17-inch screens, capable of resolutions up to 1,600 × 1,200. (The resolution is the number of pixels – dots of light – that make up the screen.)

System unit – the box containing the 'works'. This may act as a base for the monitor, or stand beside it, as in the illustration, or on the floor beneath.

On the front you should be able to see the front panels of a floppy disk drive and a CD-ROM drive, and two buttons – one is the on/off button, the other the reset button.

At the back you will find a number of sockets and connections, most with cables plugged into them.

Inside, and best left to the experts, are the power supply, the CD-ROM, floppy disk and hard disk drives, and the main circuit board (the motherboard) containing the main processor, the memory and other chips; plus a sound card, graphics card, modem and other circuit boards.

Keyboard – though mainly for entering text and numbers, the keys can also be used for controlling software, as you will see.

Mouse – used for controlling the cursor on screen, allowing you to select items, start programs, draw pictures, and more.

There will also normally be speakers and a printer, and possibly a scanner, attached.

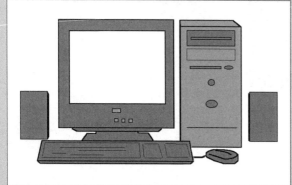

For your information

A portable or laptop PC is in practice the same as a desktop model, except that the screen is in the lid and the system unit is in the base of the keyboard. There will usually be some form of touch pad or mini-joystick in the keyboard to use in place of a mouse.

Windows is an operating system – and more. An operating system handles the interaction between the processor and the screen, memory, mouse, disk drives, printer and other equipment. It is a bridge between the hardware of the computer and the applications – such as word processing or spreadsheet programs. Whatever hardware you are using, if it has a version of Windows, it can run any application written for that or for earlier versions of Windows. (This book assumes that you are using Windows XP – but if you have an earlier version, such as 98 or Me, the differences are not very great.)

Start up

1 Turn on the PC.

2 If the monitor has its own switch, turn it on.

3 Various messages and images will appear to let you know that things are happening.

4 If you are on a network, you will need to log on – to enter your user name and password.

5 After a few more minutes' wait while the last files are loaded and the system configured for your use, the Desktop screen will appear.

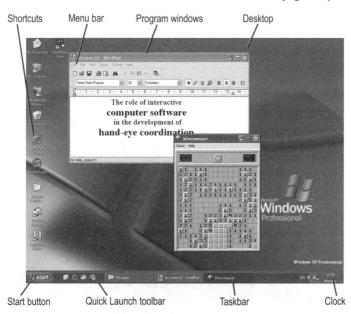

Shortcuts   Menu bar   Program windows   Desktop

Start button   Quick Launch toolbar   Taskbar   Clock

Shortcuts – instant access to programs. You can create shortcuts.

Menu bar – gives access to a program's commands.

Desktop – you can change the background picture or pattern and its colours.

Program windows – adjust their size and placing to suit yourself.

Start button – opens the Start menu, from where you should be able to start any program on your PC.

Quick Launch toolbar – a quick way to start key programs.

Taskbar – when a program is running, it has a button here. Click on a button to open its window and bring it to the front of the desktop.

Clock – optional, but handy.

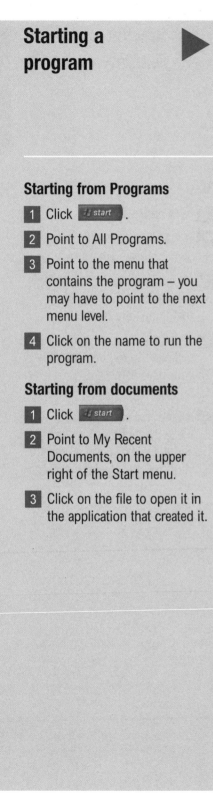

Starting a program

Starting from Programs

1. Click **start**.

2. Point to All Programs.

3. Point to the menu that contains the program – you may have to point to the next menu level.

4. Click on the name to run the program.

Starting from documents

1. Click **start**.

2. Point to My Recent Documents, on the upper right of the Start menu.

3. Click on the file to open it in the application that created it.

The programs already on your PC, and virtually all of those that you install later, will have an entry in the All Programs part of the Start menu. Selecting one from here will run the program, ready for you to start work.

A program can also be run by selecting a document that was created by it. Links to the documents used most recently are stored in the My Recent Documents folder, which can also be opened from the Start menu.

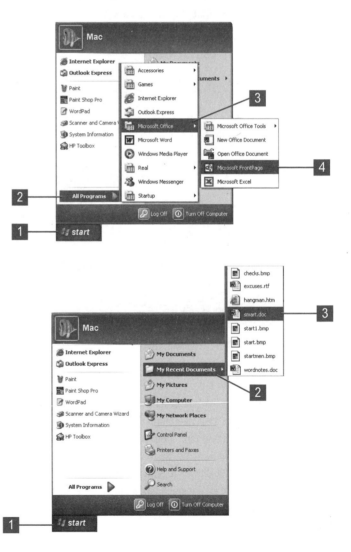

Word processing is one of the most popular uses of computers, and not surprising. Word processing puts well presented, neatly formatted, correctly spelled documents in the reach of everyone.

Windows XP comes with its own word processor – WordPad. This does not have the full scope of a professional package, such as Word, but it has a good range of formatting facilities. You can set selected text in any font, size or colour, add emphasis with bold, italics and <u>underline</u>, indent paragraphs or set their alignment, and even insert pictures, clip art, charts and many other types of objects. WordPad has all you need for writing letters, essays, memos, reports and the like. Could you write a book on it? Possibly, as long as it had a simple layout and you were happy to create the contents list and index by hand.

Most of us, most of the time, use only a fraction of the facilities of full-blown word-processors. It is often more efficient to use WordPad – because it is simpler, faster to load and to run, and faster to learn!

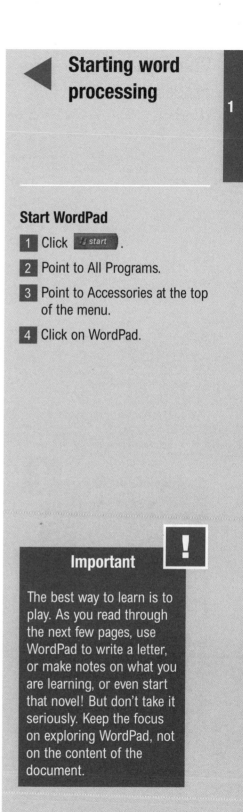

Start WordPad

1 Click **start**.

2 Point to All Programs.

3 Point to Accessories at the top of the menu.

4 Click on WordPad.

Important !

The best way to learn is to play. As you read through the next few pages, use WordPad to write a letter, or make notes on what you are learning, or even start that novel! But don't take it seriously. Keep the focus on exploring WordPad, not on the content of the document.

Starting word processing (cont.)

Entering text

All word-processors have word wrap. Don't press [Enter] as you get close to the right margin. WordPad will sense when a word is going to go over the end of a line and wrap it round to the start of the next. The only time you should press [Enter] is at the end of a paragraph or to create a blank line. If you change the margins of the page or the size of the font, WordPad will shuffle the text to fit, word wrapping as it goes.

Selecting text

- A block of text – anything from a single character to the whole document – is selected when it is highlighted. Once selected the text can be formatted, copied, deleted or moved.

- The simplest way to select text is to drag the mouse pointer over it. Take care if some of the text is below the visible area, as the scrolling can run away with you!

- A good alternative is to click the insertion point into place at the start of the block you want to select, then hold down [Shift] and use the arrow keys to move the highlight to the end of the block.

- When setting alignment or indents, which can only apply to whole paragraphs, it is enough to place the insertion point – the flashing vertical line where you type – into the paragraph.

- Double-click anywhere in a word to select it.

- Triple-click anywhere in a paragraph to select it.

Deleting errors

To correct mistakes, press [Backspace] to remove the last character you typed, or select the unwanted text and press either [Backspace] or [Delete].

You can do formatting in two ways – either select existing text and apply the format to it, or set up the format and then start typing. Either way, the formats are selected in the same way.

Use the Formatting toolbar when you want to change one aspect of the formatting – just click on the appropriate button or select from the drop-down lists.

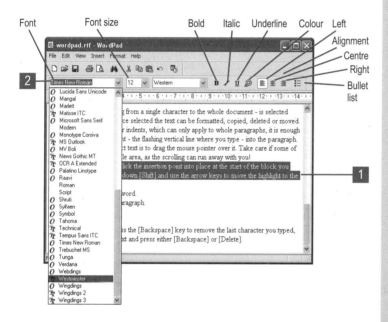

1 Select the text or go to where the new format is to start.

2 Use the Formatting tools.

Click on a button to apply or remove its formatting.

Or click the arrow beside the button to display its options and select one from the list or palette.

Important

!

Keep experimenting! Try to find a place to use every different type of formatting option.

Formatting with the Font dialogue box

Use the Font dialogue box when you want to define several aspects of the font at the same time, or if you want the rarely used strikeout effect.

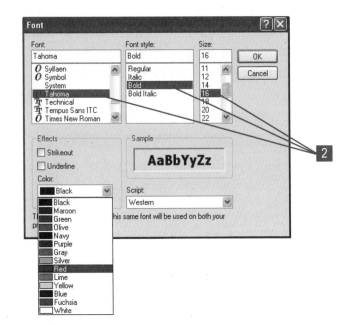

1 Select Font… from the Format menu.

2 Define the format and click OK .

Anything you type into WordPad – or most other applications – is lost when you close the application unless you save the document as a file on a disk.

The first time that you save a file, you have to specify where to put it and what to call it. If you then edit it and want to store it again, you can use a simple File > Save to resave it with the same name in the same place, overwriting the old file. If you edit a file and want to keep the old copy and the new one, then you can use File > Save As and save the new version under a different name.

In WordPad – again, as in many applications – you can save a file in several ways. The default is Rich Text Format, which can be read by most word-processors and many other applications. You can also save the words, without the formatting, by using one of the text formats.

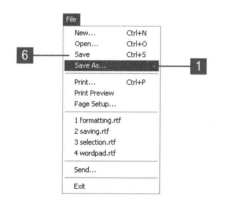

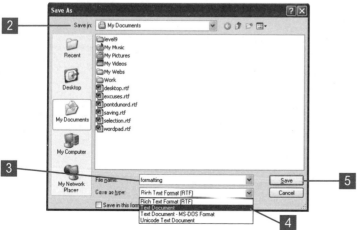

To save a new file

1 Open the File menu and select Save As…

2 Select the Save In folder.

3 Type in a Name to identify the file clearly.

4 Change the Save as type if necessary.

5 Click [Save].

Resaving a file

6 Open the File menu and select Save.

or

7 Click save on the toolbar.

! Important

If you open a Word document in WordPad, you can save it again in Word format.

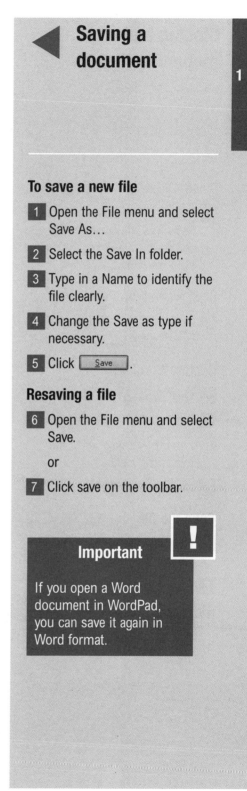

Closing and reopening files ▶

Once a document has been saved as a file it can be reopened again whenever you want to add to it or edit it, or print out another copy. Just to prove this, we'll close the document – and close WordPad for good measure – then reopen it.

Close a file

1 Open the File menu and select New. This will close the file and clear the workspace ready for a new document.

Shut down WordPad

2 Open the File menu and select Exit or click ☒.

Restart WordPad

3 Click ⊞ start .

4 Point to All Programs.

5 Point to Accessories at the top of the menu.

6 Click on WordPad.

Open the file

7 Open the File menu and select Open.

8 Locate and select your file.

9 Click Open .

In almost every Windows applications there are two ways to print a document:

Click the [Print] toolbar button to print one copy of the whole document, using the default printer.

Open the Print dialogue box to print selected pages, or set the number of copies, or control the quality of the printing.

Here's how printing works in WordPad. Use it to print your new file.

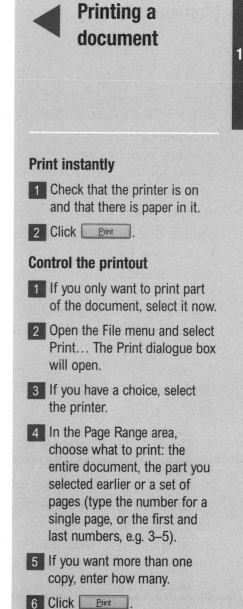

Timesaver tip

If you only want the printout for your reference, click the Preference button to open a dialogue box where you can control the quality of the printing. Set it to Draft and the document will be printed about twice as fast as usual – and it will use less ink!

Print instantly

1 Check that the printer is on and that there is paper in it.

2 Click [Print].

Control the printout

1 If you only want to print part of the document, select it now.

2 Open the File menu and select Print... The Print dialogue box will open.

3 If you have a choice, select the printer.

4 In the Page Range area, choose what to print: the entire document, the part you selected earlier or a set of pages (type the number for a single page, or the first and last numbers, e.g. 3–5).

5 If you want more than one copy, enter how many.

6 Click [Print].

Managing files ▶

My Computer is the tool that we use for managing the files on our disks. Start My Computer from its Desktop icon or the Start menu.

The main part of the window shows the contents of the current drive or folder. At first it shows the drives and main folders on your computer.

To see what's in a drive or folder, double-click on its icon. A new window will open to display its contents.

When you have finished with a window, click ⊠ to close it.

The file and folder display can fill the whole of the window, or the left part of it may be used for other purposes. The default setting – what you see if you haven't done anything to change the original setup of Windows – is to show the Common Tasks pane here. You will see later how this can be closed or replaced by the Explorer Bar.

All the commands can be reached through the Menu bar, but those that are used most often can also be reached through toolbar buttons.

There are three toolbars for exploring your PC:

■ The Address bar, which shows the current folder and can be used to move around the system.
■ The Status bar shows information about the objects in the folder or any selected ones.
■ The Standard toolbar with buttons for all the essential jobs.

The Standard toolbar

Back ·   Go back to previous folder

⊙ ·   Go to next folder

↥   Go to parent folder

Search   Search for files (page 80)

Folders   Switch between Folder List and Common Tasks

▦ ·   Alternative views of files (page 97)

Status bar

Standard toolbar

Address bar

Common Tasks pane

Click to expand/ collapse the display of items

Explorer bar

You can open the Explorer Bar on the left of the window to display the folder list. (It can also be used for Search, Favorites and History – all of which are to do with the internet. We'll ignore them just now.) The Folders list is useful.

View the folders

1. Open the View menu, point to Explorer Bar and select Folders.

   or

2. Click [Folders].

3. In the Folders list, ⊞ to the left shows that a drive or folder contains a lower level of folders.

4. Click ⊞ to bring the next level of folders into view. The icon changes to ⊟.

5. Click ⊟ when you want to hide the lower levels of folders again.

6. Click on a folder name to select it and to list its files and folders in the main part of the display.

Using Paint

There are essentially two ways to draw an image on a computer. In applications like Microsoft Draw (supplied with Word and other Office programs), the picture is made up of lines, circles, text notes, etc. each of which remain separate, and can be moved, deleted, recoloured or resized at any point.

Paint is the graphics software that comes with Windows. It uses the alternative approach. Here the image is produced by applying colour to a background, with each new line overwriting anything that may be beneath. Using this type of graphics software is very like real painting. You can wipe out a mistake while the paint is still wet, but as soon as it has dried it is fixed on the canvas – though Paint allows you to undo the last move.

Start Paint

1. Click **start** to open the Start menu.
2. Point to All Programs, to open the list of programs. Click on Accessories – it should be near the top.
3. In the Accessories menu, click on Paint.

See also

You can find out about Microsoft Draw in Chapter 6.

! Important

Remember that you've got to use it if you want to learn it! Run Paint and practice the techniques that are covered in these next few pages. You can easily rub out your mistakes, or if it is a real mess, start again from scratch. (Open the File menu and select New to restart.)

Paint can easily be used to produce simple diagrams, or to edit images captured from the screen.

Use the Text toolbar to format text – turn it on via the View menu.

The Toolbox

There is a simple but adequate set of tools. A little experimentation will show how they all work. Play with them! Release your inner Picasso! The notes here and on the next page may help.

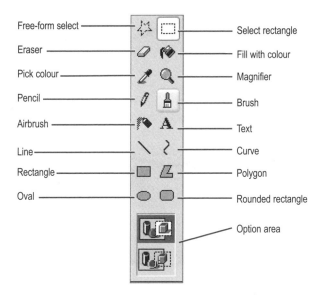

Free-form select — Select rectangle
Eraser — Fill with colour
Pick colour — Magnifier
Pencil — Brush
Airbrush — Text
Line — Curve
Rectangle — Polygon
Oval — Rounded rectangle
— Option area

The options depend upon the tool:

- Free-form/rectangle select and Text – transparent or opaque background
- Eraser and Airbrush – size
- Magnifier – level 2×, 6× or 8×
- Brush – size and shape
- Line and curve – thickness
- Rectangle, Polygon and Oval – outline or fill only, or both

To use the Erase, Pencil, Brush or Airbrush: click to leave a dot or blob; drag to create a line.

To draw a line: click where the line is to start and drag the end into position – you can move the line as long as you keep the button held down.

To draw a rectangle or oval: click at one corner of where the shape is to go and drag to the opposite corner. The shape will be drawn in the current line thickness – switch to the Line tool first if you want to change this.

Did you know?

If you hold down [Shift] when drawing, it makes ovals into circles; rectangles into squares and only allows lines to be drawn at 0°, 45° and 90°.

Using Paint (cont.)

1 Draw a line between the points where the curve will start and end.

2 Click or drag to create the first curve – exaggerate the curve as it will be reduced at the next stage.

3 Drag out the second curve now – as long as the mouse button is down, the line will flex to follow the cursor.

or

4 For a single curve, just click at the end of the line.

Drawing a curve

The curved line tool is a bit trickier than the rest. Even when you have the hang of how this works, it will still take you several goes to get a line right!

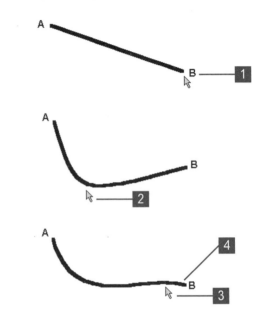

Timesaver tip

Press [Prt Sc] to copy the whole screen to the Clipboard, or [Alt] + [Prt Sc] to copy the active window. The image can be pasted into Paint and saved. That's how the screenshots were produced for this book.

Using colours

The colour palette is used in almost the same way in all Windows programs. You can select a colour from the palette – use the left button for the foreground colour and the right button for the background – or mix your own. Remember that you are mixing light, not paint.

- red and green make yellow
- green and blue make cyan
- blue and red make magenta
- red, green and blue make white

the more you use, the lighter the colour.

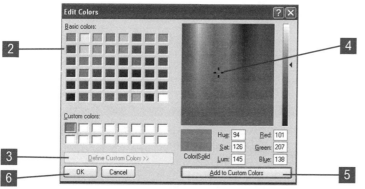

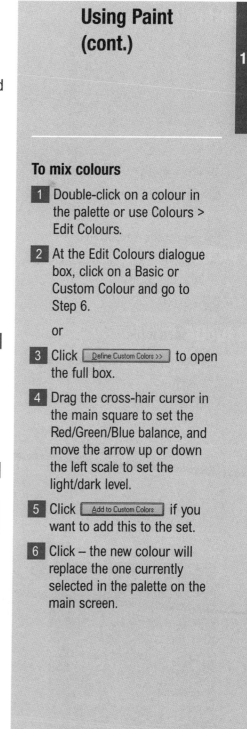

Using Paint (cont.)

1

To mix colours

1 Double-click on a colour in the palette or use Colours > Edit Colours.

2 At the Edit Colours dialogue box, click on a Basic or Custom Colour and go to Step 6.

or

3 Click [Define Custom Colors >>] to open the full box.

4 Drag the cross-hair cursor in the main square to set the Red/Green/Blue balance, and move the arrow up or down the left scale to set the light/dark level.

5 Click [Add to Custom Colors] if you want to add this to the set.

6 Click – the new colour will replace the one currently selected in the palette on the main screen.

Did you know?

If you hold down the right mouse button, lines are drawn in the background colour instead of the foreground colour.

If you hold it down while using the eraser, it replaces any current foreground colour with background colour.

Saving an image ▶

If you want to keep your image, or use it in another application, you need to save it as a file. The process is very similar to saving a document in WordPad.

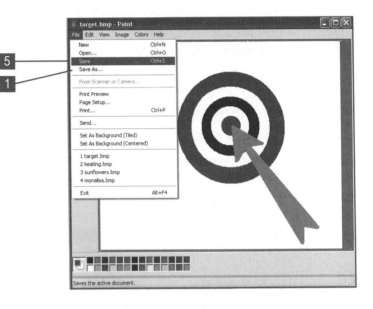

To save a new file

1 Open the File menu and select Save As…

2 Select the Save In folder.

3 Type in a File name to identify the file clearly.

4 Click [Save].

To resave a file

5 Open the File menu and select Save.

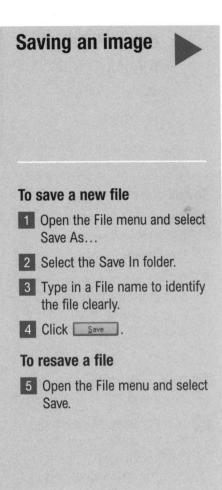

! Important

In the next section you will need an image that you can insert into the text document you created earlier. Try to draw something suitable, and save it.

? Did you know?

Paint can save images in half a dozen different file formats, but the default .BMP (bitmap) does the job very nicely for our purposes just now. There's more on graphic file formats in Chapter 6.

Word processors can handle other things as well as text. Even WordPad, which is probably the simplest word processor around, can cope with images. Try it now. Insert the image that you just created into your text file.

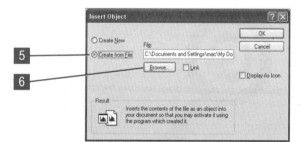

Insert an image

1 Run WordPad if it is not already open (see page 5).

2 Open the file you created earlier.

3 Click into the document at the point where you want to place the image.

4 Open the Insert menu and select Object.

5 Click Create from File.

6 Click Browse... .

Inserting an image into a document (cont.)

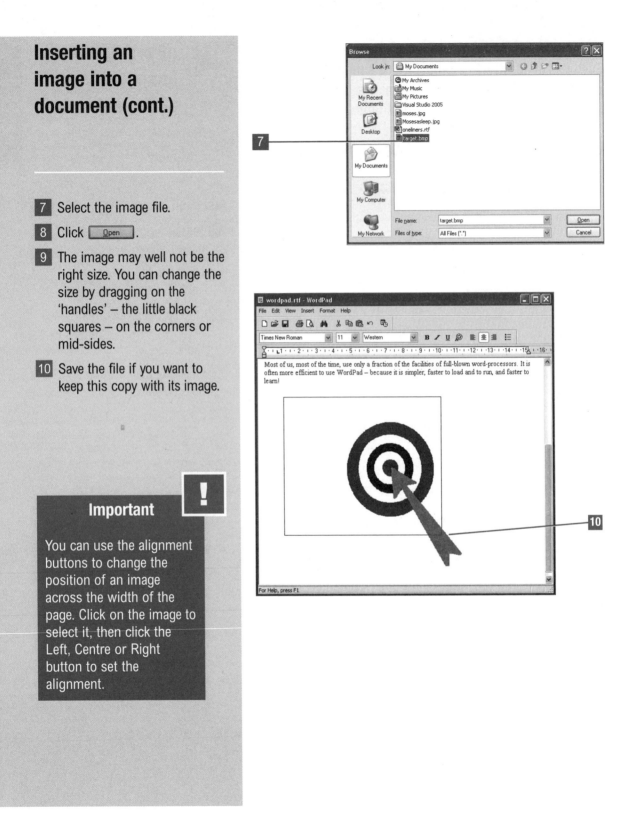

7 Select the image file.

8 Click [Open].

9 The image may well not be the right size. You can change the size by dragging on the 'handles' – the little black squares – on the corners or mid-sides.

10 Save the file if you want to keep this copy with its image.

Important

You can use the alignment buttons to change the position of an image across the width of the page. Click on the image to select it, then click the Left, Centre or Right button to set the alignment.

When you have finished work on your computer, you must shut it down properly, and not just turn it off. This is essential. During a working session, application programs and Windows XP itself may have created temporary files – and any data files that you have been editing may still be open in memory and not yet written safely to disk. A proper shutdown closes and stores open files and removes unwanted ones.

Restart

The Turn off computer dialogue box offers a Restart option. You may need this after installing new software or hardware. There may also be a Stand By or Hibernate option. This will turn off the main power-using parts of your system – the hard drive, monitor and fans – but leave the RAM memory active, and files and programs open, so that you can start up quickly when you return.

Systems differ – check your PC's handbook to find out about its stand by facilities.

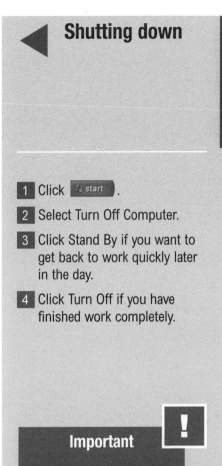

1 Click **start** .

2 Select Turn Off Computer.

3 Click Stand By if you want to get back to work quickly later in the day.

4 Click Turn Off if you have finished work completely.

Important

!

If you simply turn off the PC, or have to use the Restart button, when it starts up again, Windows will offer to check your hard drive(s) in case there is a problem. The check only takes a few moments and is normally worth doing.

Windows essentials

2

Introduction

Windows XP is an operating system – and more. An operating system handles the low-level interaction between the processor and the screen, memory, mouse, disk drives, printer and other peripherals. Windows XP has drivers (control programs) for all PC-compatible processors and virtually all of the many PC peripherals on the market. The operating system is a bridge between the hardware of the computer and its applications – such as word-processors and spreadsheets. As a result, whoever manufactured your PC and whatever type it is, as long as it can run the Windows XP operating system, it can run any Windows XP application. (It will also be able to run applications written for earlier versions of Windows.)

Although the operating system is the most important part of Windows, most of it is invisible. The visible part is the screen or Desktop. Windows is a graphical system. It uses icons (small images) to represent programs and files, and visual displays to show what is happening inside your PC. Many of the routine jobs are done by clicking on, dragging or otherwise manipulating these images, using the mouse or keyboard.

Windows is multi-tasking – it can run any number of programs at once. Each program runs in a separate area of the screen – a window – and these can be resized, moved, minimized or overlapped however you like. In practice, only a few will normally be active at the same time but that is more a reflection of the human inability to do several jobs simultaneously! A typical example of multi-tasking would be one program downloading material from the internet and another printing a long report, while you wrote a letter in a third.

This chapter covers the basic skills and concepts of working with Windows. You will learn how to use the mouse and the keyboard to select from menus, make choices, run programs and control the window layouts. You will also find out how to get help and how to cope when things go wrong.

Exploring the Desktop

Windows is a Graphical User Interface (or GUI, pronounced gooey). What this means is that you work mainly by using the mouse to point at and click on symbols on the screen, rather than by typing commands. It is largely intuitive – i.e. the obvious thing to do is probably the right thing – and it is tolerant of mistakes. Many can be corrected as long as you tackle them straight away, and many others can be corrected easily, even after time has passed.

One of the key ideas behind the design of Windows is that you should treat the screen as you would a desk, which is why Windows refers to the screen as the desktop. This is where you lay out your papers, books and tools, and you can arrange them to suit your own way of working. You may want to have more than one set of papers on the desktop at a time – so Windows lets you run several programs at once. You may want to have all your papers visible, for comparing or transferring data; you may want to concentrate on one, but have the others to hand. These – and other arrangements – are all possible.

Each program runs in its own window, and these can be arranged side by side, overlapping, or with the one you are working on filling the desktop and the others tucked out of the way, but still instantly accessible.

Just as there are many ways of arranging your desktop, so there are many ways of working with it – in fact, you are sometimes spoilt for choice!

It's your desktop. How you arrange it, and how you use it is up to you. This book will show you the simplest ways to use Windows XP effectively.

- What you see on screen when you start Windows depends upon your Desktop settings and the shortcuts – the icons that you can click on to start programs – you are using.
- What the screen looks like once you are into your working session, is infinitely variable.
- Certain principles always apply and certain things are always there. It is the fact that all Windows applications share a common approach that makes Windows so easy to use.

Shortcuts   Menu bar   Program windows   Desktop

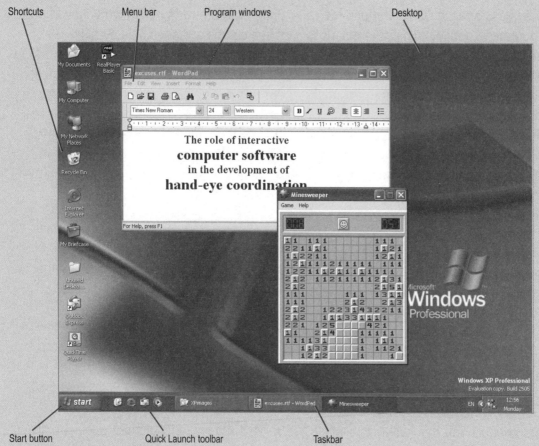

Start button   Quick Launch toolbar   Taskbar

Shortcuts – instant access to programs. You can create your own shortcuts.

Desktop – you can change the background picture or pattern and its colours.

Menu bar – gives access to a program's commands.

Program windows – adjust their size and placing to suit yourself.

Start button – you should be able to start any program on your PC from its menu.

Quick Launch toolbar – a quick way to start key programs.

Taskbar – when a program is running, it has a button here. Click on a button to open its window and bring it to the front of the desktop.

Most Windows XP operations can be handled quite happily by the mouse alone, leaving the keyboard for data entry. However, keys are necessary for some jobs, and if you prefer typing to mousing, it is possible to do most jobs from the keyboard. The relevant ones are shown here.

The function keys

Some operations can be run from these – for instance, [F1] starts up the Help system in any Windows application.

The control sets

The Arrow keys can often be used instead of the mouse for moving the cursor. Above them are more movement keys, which will let you jump around in text. [Insert] and [Delete] are also here.

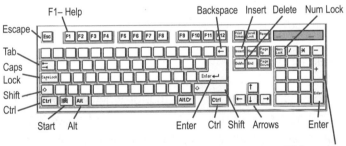

Key guide

[Esc] – to escape from trouble. Use it to cancel bad choices.

[Tab] – move between objects on screen.

[Caps Lock] – only put this on when you want to type a lot of capitals. The Caps Lock light shows if it is on.

[Shift] – use it for capitals and the symbols on the number keys.

[Ctrl] or [Control] – used with other keys to give keystroke alternatives to mouse commands.

▨ – same as clicking Start on the screen.

[Alt] – used, like [Ctrl], with other keys.

[Backspace] – rubs out the character to the left of the text cursor.

[Enter] – used at the end of a piece of text or to start an operation.

[Delete] – deletes files, folders and screen objects. Use with care.

Controlling the mouse

You can't do much in Windows until you have tamed the mouse. It is used for locating the cursor, for selecting from menus, highlighting, moving and changing the size of objects, and much more. It won't bite, but it will wriggle until you have shown it who is in charge.

The mouse and the cursor

There are two main types of mice.

One type has a ball beneath. Moving the mouse rolls the ball inside it. The ball turns the sensor rollers and these transmit the movement to the cursor. To control this type of mouse effectively you need a mouse mat or a thin pad of paper – it won't run well on a hard surface.

The other type uses infrared to scan the area beneath and work out which way the mouse has moved. This type needs some kind of image or pattern beneath it – it won't know where it is on a plain surface.

With either type:

■ If you reach the edge of the mat or whatever you are using as a mouse run, so that you cannot move the cursor any further, pick up the mouse and plonk it back into the middle.

■ You can set up the mouse so that when the mouse is moved faster, the cursor moves further. Watch out for this when working on other people's machines.

Mouse actions

■ Point – move the cursor with your fingers off the buttons.

■ Click – the left button to select a file, menu item or other object.

■ Right-click (click the right button) to open a menu of commands that can be applied to the object beneath the pointer.

- Double-click to run programs. You can set the gap between clicks to suit yourself.
- Drag – keep the left button down while moving the mouse. Used for resizing, drawing and similar jobs.
- Drag and drop – drag an object and release the left button when it is in the right place. Used for moving objects.

Controlling the mouse (cont.)

2

See also

Adjusting the mouse, page 179 to find out how to adjust the responsiveness of the mouse to suit your hand.

Using the Start menu

▶

Clicking on [Start] at the bottom left of the screen opens the Start menu. Yours will look a little different to mine – you can adapt the Start menu, and it will adapt to you automatically.

At the top left are links to your browser and email software (normally Internet Explorer and Outlook Express).

Beneath these are links to your most-used programs – initially this will be empty.

At the bottom left is the All Programs link (see the next page).

At the top right are links to My Documents, My Pictures and other folders where documents and files are commonly stored.

My Recent Documents holds a list of your latest documents. Selecting one from this list will run the relevant application and open the file for you to work on.

You can configure your PC through the Control Panel (Chapter 7). You may have a link to the Printers and Faxes, and/or a Connect To link which leads to your connections for going online.

Help and Support starts the Help system (page 41).

Use Search to track down files on your computer, or to find web pages or people on the internet.

Log off... allows the current user to stop using the PC – and for a new user to start – without turning it off.

Turn Off Computer is the only safe way to shut down the PC.

Jargon buster

Windows uses '**document**' to mean any file created by any application. A word-processed report is obviously a document, but so is a picture file from a graphics package, a data file from a spreadsheet, a video clip, sound file – in fact, any file produced by any program.

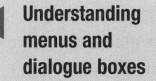

There are many situations where you have to specify a filename or an option. Sometimes you have to type in what you want, but in most cases, it only takes a click of the mouse or a couple of keystrokes.

Menus

In any Windows application, you can find all of its commands and options on the menus, with each menu containing a set of related commands. Menus drop down from the menu bar. To make it drop down, click on its name with the mouse, or press [Alt] (the key marked 'Alt') and the underlined letter – usually the initial.

Click or press [Alt] + [V]

Toggle – this option is turned on

Point to open sub-menu

Dialogue box will open

To select an item from a menu, click on it or type its underlined letter.

Some items are toggles. Selecting them turns an option on or off. ✔ beside the name shows that the option is on.

▶ after an item shows that another menu leads from it.

If you select an item with three dots ... after it, a dialogue box will open to get more information from you.

Dialogue boxes

These vary, but will usually have these buttons:

⬚ OK ⬚ click when you have set the options, selected the file or whatever. This confirms your choices and closes the box.

⬚ Apply ⬚ click to fix the options selected so far, but keep the box open for further work.

⬚ Cancel ⬚ click if you decide the choices are all wrong.

⬚?⬚ to get Help on items in the box.

Tabs and panels

Some dialogue boxes have several sets of options in them, each on a separate panel. These are identified by tabs at the top. Click on a tab to bring its panel to the front. Usually clicking ⬚ OK ⬚ on any panel will close the whole box. Use ⬚ Apply ⬚ when you have finished with one panel but want to explore others before closing.

Understanding menus and dialogue boxes (cont.)

Check boxes

These are used where there are several options, and you can use as many as you like at the same time.

✔ in the box shows that the option has been selected.

If the box is grey and the caption faint, the option is 'greyed out' – not available at that time for the selected item.

These are selected

Radio buttons

These are used for either/or options. Only one of the set can be selected.

The selected option is shown by a black blob in the middle.

This one is selected

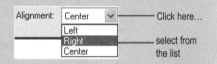

Drop-down lists

If a slot has a down arrow button on its right, click the button to drop down a list.

Click on an item in the list to select.

Alignment: Center — Click here...
Left
Right — select from
Center — the list

Timesaver tip

Some commands have keyboard shortcuts. These are sometimes the [F...] keys, but often [Ctrl] + a letter. If there is a shortcut it will usually be shown on the menu after the command name.

If you click the right button on almost any object on screen in Windows XP, a short menu will open beside it. This contains a set of commands and options that can be applied to the object.

What is on the menu depends upon the type of object and its context – hence the name. Two are shown here to give an idea of the possibilities.

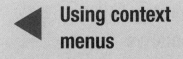
Open
New
Print
Open With ▶
Send To ▶
Cut
Copy
Create Shortcut
Delete
Rename
Properties

Files can be opened, sent to a removable disk or off in the mail, and deleted – amongst other things.

Toolbars ▶
Adjust Date/Time
Customize Notifications...
Cascade Windows
Tile Windows Horizontally
Tile Windows Vertically
Show the Desktop
Task Manager
Lock the Taskbar
Properties

The Clock can be adjusted, and as it is on the Taskbar, you can also arrange the screen display from this menu.

Working with windows ▶

The window frame

The frame contains all the controls you need for adjusting the display.

1 The frame edge has a control system built into it. When a window is in Restore mode – i.e. smaller than full-screen – you can drag on the edge to make it larger or smaller.

2 The title bar is to remind you of where you are – in the active application (the one you are using) it is blue; in any other open applications it is grey. You can drag on the bar to move a window.

3 The Maximize, Minimize and Restore buttons change the display mode. Only one of Maximize and Restore will be visible at any one time.

4 The Close button is one of several ways to close a window and the program that was running in it.

5 The Control menu icon looks different in every application but clicking on it will always open the Control menu which can be used for changing the screen mode or closing the window.

6 The Menu bar usually sits just below the Title bar in an application's window, and contains the names of its drop-down menus.

7 The Scroll bars are present on the right side and bottom of the frame if the display contained by the window is too big to fit within it. The Sliders in the Scroll bars show you where your view is, relative to the overall display. Moving these allows you to view a different part of the display. (See Scrolling, page 35.)

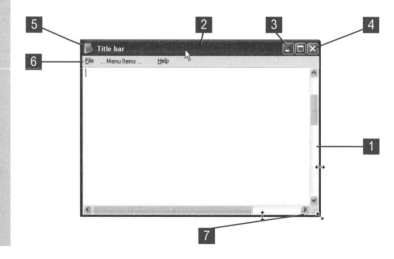

What you can see in a window is often only part of the story. The working area of the application may well be much larger. If there are scroll bars on the side and/or bottom of the window, this tells you that there is more material outside the frame. The scroll bars let you pull some of this material into view.

Arrow buttons

Working area

Sliders

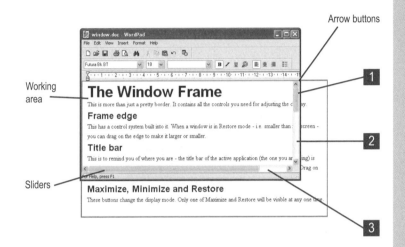

Scrolling in a window

1 Drag the slider to scroll the view in the window. Drag straight along the bar or it won't work!

2 Click an arrow button to edge the slider towards it. Hold down for a slow continuous scroll.

3 Click on the bar beside the slider to make it jump towards where you are clicking.

Changing the window mode

All programs are displayed on screen in windows, and these can normally have three modes:

- Maximized – filling the whole screen.
- Minimized – not displayed, though still present as a button on the Taskbar. Restore – adjustable in size and in position.

Clicking on the buttons in the top right corner of the frame is the simplest way to switch between Maximize and Restore modes, and to Minimize a window.

A window in Restore mode   A Maximized window   The current window is highlighted

Minimized – not visible except for this.

Did you know?

You can change window modes using the the Control menu. Click the icon at the top left of the window to open it. This menu came from a variable size window, so Restore is shown in grey as it does not apply. One from a full-screen window would have Move, Size and Maximize in grey.

You can open the menu using the keys:

[Alt]+[Space] opens the Control menu of an application.

[Alt]+[–] (minus) opens the Control menu of a document.

To make a window full-screen: Click ▣.

To shrink a window to a Taskbar button: Click ▬ To redisplay it, click on its Taskbar button.

To restore a window to variable size: Click ▣.

Timesaver tip

When you minimize a document window, within an application, it shrinks to a tiny title bar, with just enough room for a name and the icons. Click Maximize or Restore to open it out again.

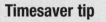

If you want to have two or more windows visible at the same time, you will have to arrange them on your desktop. There are Windows tools that will do it for you, or you can do it yourself.

If you right-click the Taskbar, its menu has options to arrange the windows on the desktop. Similar options are on the Window menu of most applications, to set the layout within the programs.

Cascade places the windows overlapping with only the title bars of the back ones showing.

Tile Windows Vertically and Tile Windows Horizontally arrange open windows side by side, or one above the other– with more than three windows, the tiling is in both directions. As the window frames take up space, the actual working area is significantly reduced. Obviously, larger, high-resolution screens are better for multi-window work, but even on a 1,280 × 1,024 display you cannot do much serious typing in a tiled window.

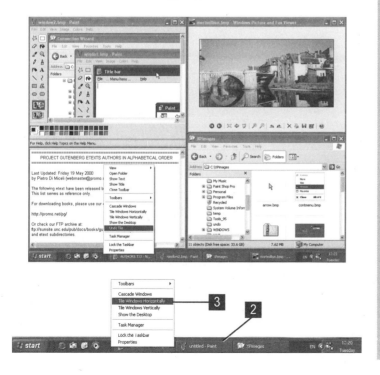

To tile windows

1 Maximize or Restore the windows that you want to include in the layout. Minimize those that you will not be using actively.

2 Right-click the Taskbar to open its menu.

3 Select Tile Windows Horizontally or Tile Windows Vertically.

4 If you only want to work in one window at a time, Maximize it, and Restore it back into the arrangement when you have done.

5 If you want to adjust the balance of the layout, you can move and resize the windows.

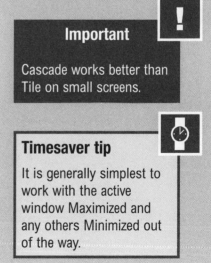

Important

Cascade works better than Tile on small screens.

Timesaver tip

It is generally simplest to work with the active window Maximized and any others Minimized out of the way.

Moving windows ▶

When a window is in Restore mode – open but not full screen – it can be moved anywhere on the screen.

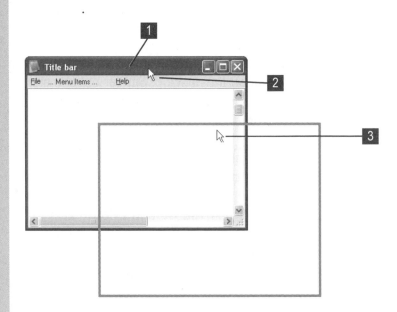

1. If the title bar isn't highlighted, click on the window to make it the active one.

2. Point at the title bar and hold the left button down.

3. Drag the window to its new position – you will only see a grey outline moving.

4. Release the button.

When a window is in Restore mode, you can change its size and shape by dragging the edges of the frame to new positions. Combined with the moving facility, this lets you arrange your desktop exactly the way you like it.

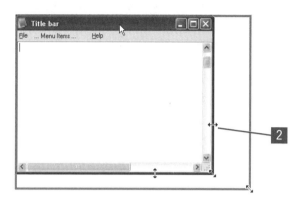

1 Move the pointer to the edge or corner that you want to pull in or out.

2 When you see the double-headed arrow, hold down the left mouse button and drag the outline to the required size.

3 Release the button.

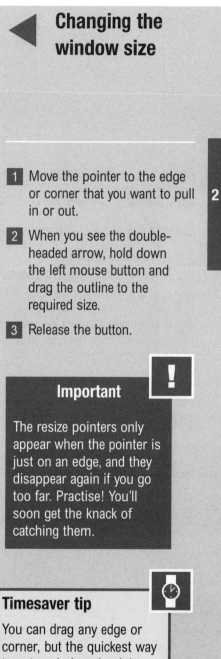

Important

!

The resize pointers only appear when the pointer is just on an edge, and they disappear again if you go too far. Practise! You'll soon get the knack of catching them.

Timesaver tip

You can drag any edge or corner, but the quickest way to get a window the right size, in the right place, is to use the bottom right size handle to set the shape, then drag the window into position.

Closing windows ▶

Closing an active window

1 Click ⊠ or press [Alt]+[F4].

Closing from the Taskbar

2 Right-click the program's Taskbar button to get its menu.

3 Select Close.

4 If you have forgotten to save your work, take the opportunity that is offered to you.

When you close a window, you close down the program that was running inside it.

If you haven't saved your work, most programs will point this out and give you a chance to save before closing.

There are at least five different ways of closing. Here are the simplest three:

■ If the window is in Maximized or Restore mode, click the close icon at the top right of the Title bar. (If your mouse control is not too good, you may well do this when you are trying to Maximize the window!)

■ If the window has been Minimized onto the Taskbar, right-click on its button to open the Control menu and use Close.

■ If you prefer working from keys, press [Alt]+[F4].

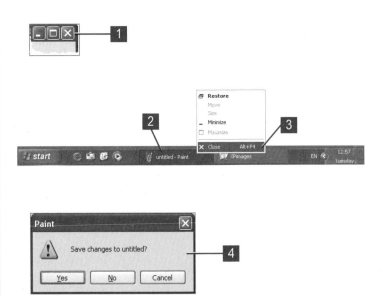

Windows XP has its own special Help and Support system. It's very comprehensive and has some excellent features, but – most unhelpfully – it looks and feels different from the standard application Help systems.

The Home page acts as a contents page. Start to browse through the Help pages from here. It will typically take you four clicks to get from a main topic heading on the Home page, through to a specific page on a Help topic.

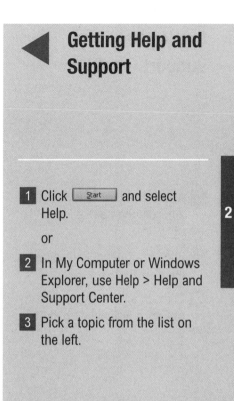

1 Click [Start] and select Help.

or

2 In My Computer or Windows Explorer, use Help > Help and Support Center.

3 Pick a topic from the list on the left.

Getting Help and Support (cont.)

4 At the next level, click ⊞ by a heading to open a list of topics.

5 Click a sub-topic to display a list of Help pages.

6 Click on a Fix a problem or Pick a task link to open its page.

Click to return to the Home page

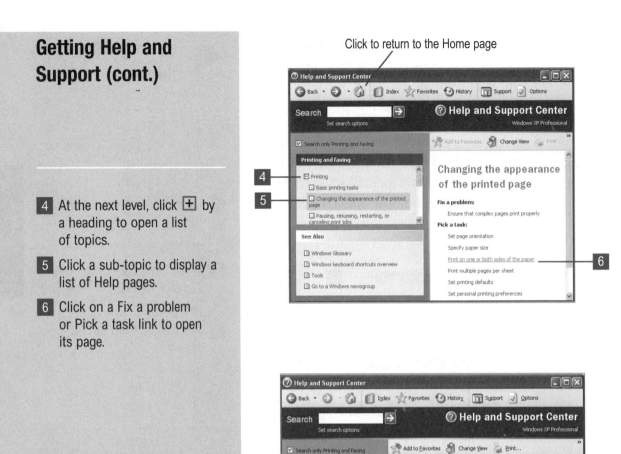

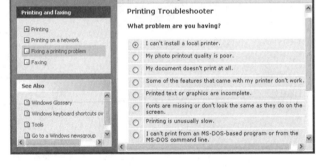

Some Help links lead to troubleshooters. These will take you through a series of questions and actions to (often) locate and solve the problem.

Though the Contents are good for getting an overview of how things work, if you want help on a specific problem – usually the case – you are better off with the Index.

This is organised through a cross-referenced list of terms. The main list is alphabetical, with sub-entries, just like the index in a book. And, as with an index in a book, you can plough through it slowly from the top, or skip through to find the words that start with the right letters. Once you find a suitable entry, you can display the list of cross-referenced topics and pick one of those.

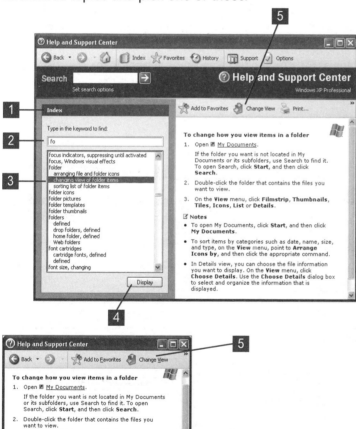

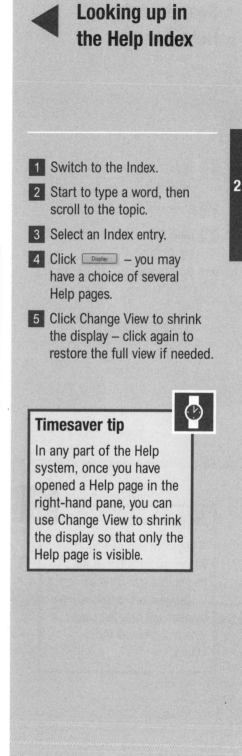

1 Switch to the Index.

2 Start to type a word, then scroll to the topic.

3 Select an Index entry.

4 Click `Display` – you may have a choice of several Help pages.

5 Click Change View to shrink the display – click again to restore the full view if needed.

Timesaver tip

In any part of the Help system, once you have opened a Help page in the right-hand pane, you can use Change View to shrink the display so that only the Help page is visible.

Searching for Help

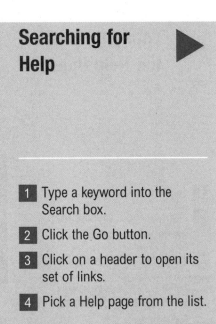

1. Type a keyword into the Search box.
2. Click the Go button.
3. Click on a header to open its set of links.
4. Pick a Help page from the list.

On the Index panel you are hunting through the titles of Help pages. On the Search panel, the system looks for matching keywords within pages.

The Search box is present on every page of the Help system. The results are grouped in three sets – click the headers to see their results.

Suggested Topics are normally the most useful. These are the pages that have been indexed by the keyword.

Full-text Search Matches are pages which contain your keywords, but these may only be passing references.

Microsoft Knowledge Base draws help from Microsoft's website and is, of course, only available if you are online.

Jargon buster

A **keyword** can be any word which might occur in the pages that you are looking for. If you give two or more, the system will only list pages which contain all those words.

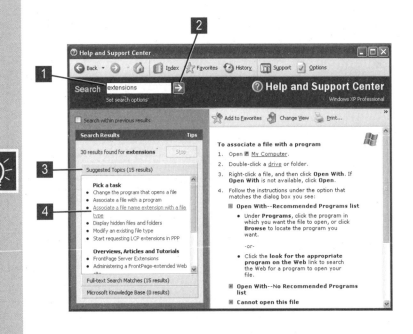

Windows XP is a pretty stable system, but things do go wrong. A 'crash' can can be at several levels.

- A program may simply misbehave – it will still run, but not respond or update the screen correctly. Close it – saving any open files – and run it again. If it still behaves badly, close down all your programs and restart the PC.
- The system will 'hang' – i.e. nothing is happening and it will not respond to the mouse or normal keyboard commands. If the [Control] + [Alt] + [Del] keystroke works, you can reach the Task Manager to close the offending application, which may get things moving again.
- You get a total lock up where it will not pick up [Control] + [Alt] + [Del]. Press the little restart button on the front of the PC. It is there for just these times!

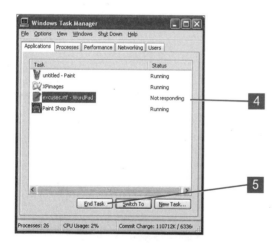

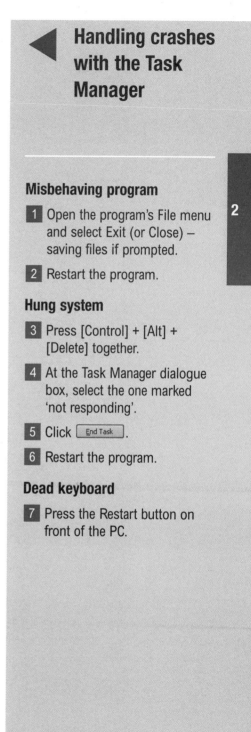

Handling crashes with the Task Manager

Misbehaving program

1 Open the program's File menu and select Exit (or Close) – saving files if prompted.

2 Restart the program.

Hung system

3 Press [Control] + [Alt] + [Delete] together.

4 At the Task Manager dialogue box, select the one marked 'not responding'.

5 Click [End Task].

6 Restart the program.

Dead keyboard

7 Press the Restart button on front of the PC.

Simple Word processing

3

Introduction

Word processing is probably the most widely used computer application, and the most widely used word processing software is Microsoft Word. You probably have Word on your machine. It is often included in 'package deals' on new PCs, and supplied ready-installed – if yours is new, and you are still exploring it, have a look for Word now. Is it on the Programs group on the Start menu? If you cannot see a 'Microsoft Word' item on the main list, is there a 'Microsoft Office' sub-menu containing Word? Word is also included in some versions of the Works software suite, which is also commonly bundled with new PCs.

If you do not have Word on your PC, don't go out and buy it unless you really need its advanced facilities, as Windows comes with a perfectly good, if slightly limited, word processor. WordPad can handle letters, reports, minutes of meetings, simple brochures and newsletters, and has much the same formatting facilities as Word. It is, in effect, a cut-down version of Word, with the same commands and toolbar buttons – but just not as many of them. In this chapter, the examples and instructions are for Word, but virtually all of them apply equally well to WordPad.

What you'll do

Explore the Word screen

Start a new document

Select text

Edit text

Undo mistakes

Emphasise text

Set fonts

Change the text size

Use the Font dialogue box

Colour your text

Align text

Set the line spacing

Define the Page Setup

Save a document

Print a document

Use Print Preview

Get Help

Find Help through the Contents

Find Help through the Index

Exploring the
Word screen

The main part of the screen forms the working area, where you type your text and insert graphics and other objects to create your documents. Around this area are:

- The Title bar, showing the name of the document, and carrying the usual Minimize, Maximize/Restore and Close application buttons.

- The Menu bar, giving you access to all of Word's many features.

- The toolbars – normally only the Standard and Formatting toolbars are open, but others can be displayed as required. The toolbars are usually on the top and side of the working area, but can be moved or floated.

- The scroll bars, used for moving around your document – just drag the sliders or click the arrows at the ends to scroll the display. At the bottom of the right scroll

bar are buttons for moving between pages; and at the left of the bottom bar are four buttons for changing the view. Click on each of these to see the effect – Normal or Print Layout views are best for most work.

- The ruler, showing the margins, indents and tabs. This is not present in some views.

- The Status Bar, showing where you are in the document, what language the spell checker is using, and the state of various toggle (on/off) options.

The area on the right of the window is sometimes occupied by the Task Pane. When you first run Word, there will be a range of options here for starting new files or opening existing ones. The Task Pane is also used for inserting clip art, formatting, the Clipboard and other functions. It can be closed when not needed.

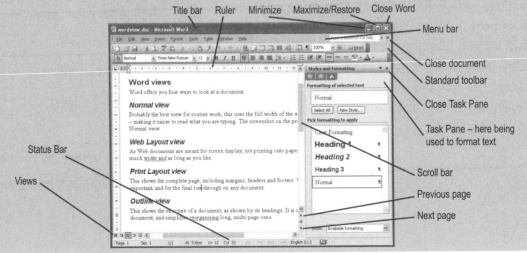

Word views

Word offers you four ways to look at a document.

Normal view

Probably the best view for routine work, this uses the full width of the window to display the text area – making it easier to read what you are typing. The screenshot below shows Word in Normal view.

Web Layout view

As Web documents are meant for screen display, not printing onto paper, this view has 'pages' that are much wider and as long as you like.

Print Layout view

This shows the complete page, including margins, headers and footers. Use it when layout is very important, and for the final run-through on any document.

Outline view

This shows the structure of a document, as shown by its headings. It is useful when planning a new document, and simplifies reorganising long, multi-page ones.

Exploring the Word screen (cont.)

To change views:

1 To switch between views, use the buttons at the bottom left of the screen.

or

2 Open the View menu.

3 Select a view

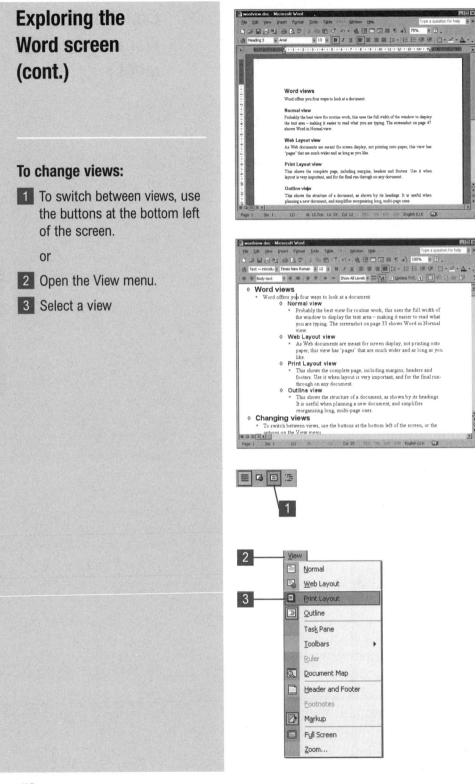

All documents start from some kind of template which sets up the basic design. That bare white page that you see when you first start Word is in fact a 'blank document' template. In this case it simply sets the page size and the fonts for the normal and heading text. Other templates may have some text or images already in place – headed paper for letters, for example – and/or have more elaborate design features or suggestions for content and layout of the items to include in the new document.

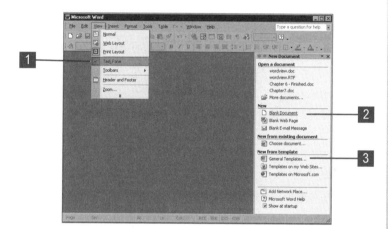

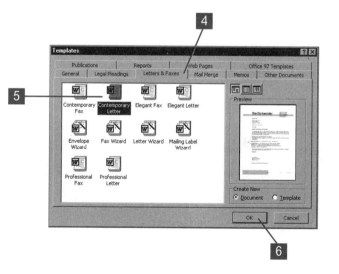

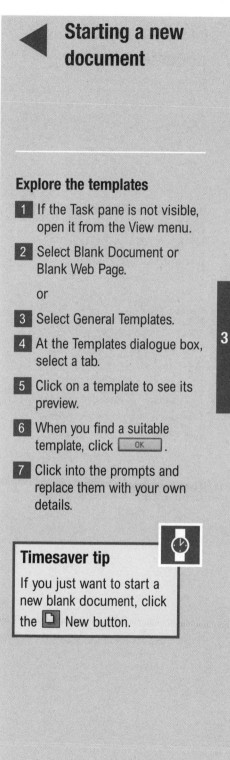

Starting a new document

Explore the templates

1. If the Task pane is not visible, open it from the View menu.

2. Select Blank Document or Blank Web Page.

   or

3. Select General Templates.

4. At the Templates dialogue box, select a tab.

5. Click on a template to see its preview.

6. When you find a suitable template, click ⬡ OK ⬡.

7. Click into the prompts and replace them with your own details.

Timesaver tip

If you just want to start a new blank document, click the ⬡ New button.

Starting a new document (cont.)

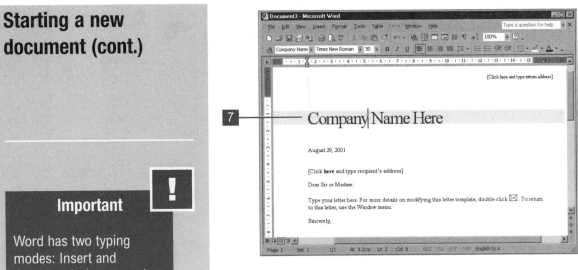

When you start typing on a blank page, the text will first appear at the top left corner and gradually fill down. In an existing document, text is placed at the insertion point – the flashing line. If this is not where you want to type, click to move the insertion point to the right place.

Before you can do any kind of editing, you must first select the text. A block of text can be any size, from one character to the whole document. How you select depends upon the size of block that you want.

To select:

■ A word – double-click anywhere in the word.
■ A line – click in the margin to the left of the line.
■ A paragraph – triple-click inside the paragraph.
■ Any other text – click at the start of the block and drag to the end.
■ Any size block – move the insertion point to the start of the block, hold down [Shift] and move to the end using keystrokes.

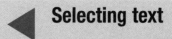
3

Click here to select the line   You can start to select at any point

My Life in Three Acts
Past
I was born when I was very young, and much has happened since. Some things I have forgotten, some I would prefer to forget, but I still remember my first bike. It had three wheels, a boot and a bell, and it went like the wind, though much noisier.

Present
I love to ...

Future
In five years' time I hope to be...

Selecting text (cont.)

Keys in Word

If you make a mistake, use [Backspace] to erase the character(s) that you have just typed.

If you spot a mistake later, click the insertion point into the text and use [Backspace] to erase to its left or [Delete] to erase to its right, or select the text and press [Delete].

To move around the text using the keys:

- [Arrows] – one character left or right, one line up or down; one word left or right if [Ctrl] is held down.
- [PgUp] – move one screenful up.
- [PgDn] – move one screenful down.
- [Home] – jump to the start of the line; or the start of the text if [Ctrl] is held down.
- [End] – jump to the end of the line; or the end of the text if [Ctrl] is held down.

Timesaver tip

If you want to select all the text, press [Ctrl] and [A].

Important

In Word the cursor is an I-beam, rather than an arrow pointer. This is to help you position it accurately in the text.

When word processing, you should never have to write anything twice. If you need to use the same words several times, text can be copied. If text is in the wrong place, it can be moved.

There are two main techniques for copying and moving text.

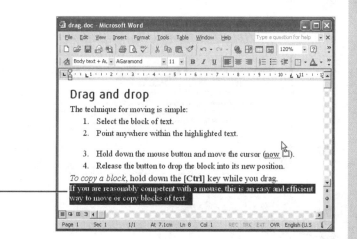

Drag and drop

If you are reasonably competent with a mouse, this is an easy and efficient way to move or copy blocks of text.

1 Select the block of text.

2 Point anywhere within the highlighted text.

3 Hold down the mouse button and move the cursor (now ⬚).

4 Release the button to drop the block into its new position.

To copy a block, hold down the [Ctrl] key while you drag.

3

Editing text (cont.)

The Edit menu of every Windows application has the commands Cut, Copy and Paste. You will also find them on the context menu that opens when you right-click on an object, and there are buttons for them on the Standard toolbar. These are used for copying and moving data within and between applications.

Cut deletes a selected block of text, picture, file or other object, but places a copy in the Clipboard.

Copy copies the selected data into the Clipboard.

Paste copies the data from the Clipboard into a different place in the same application, or into a different application – as long as this can handle data in that format.

The data remains in the Clipboard until new data is copied into it, or until Windows is shut down.

Cut, Copy and Paste

1 Select the block of text.

2 Click [image].

   or

3 Open the Edit menu or right-click and select Cut or Copy.

4 Place the cursor where you want the text.

5 Click [image].

   or

6 Open the Edit menu or right-click and select Paste.

Jargon buster

Windows has a special part of memory known as the **Clipboard**, which can be used for storing any kind of data – text, images, spreadsheets, complete files or small selected chunks. It can be used not just for copying or moving data within an application, but also between applications as the Clipboard can be accessed from any program.

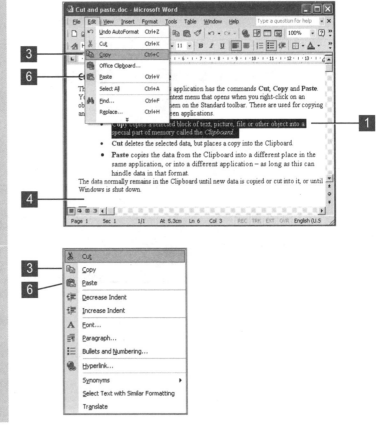

Cut and Paste

The Cut operation is the same as Copy except that it deletes the selected block of text, picture, file or whatever object, when it places a copy in the Clipboard.

Editing text (cont.)

Cut and Paste

The Cut operation is the same as Copy except that deletes the selected block of text, picture, file or whatev...   copy in the Clipboard

To move text:
1. Select the block of t
2. Open the Edit menu   Cut.
3. Place the cursor wh
4. Open the Edit menu   aste.

Cut
Copy
Paste

Font...
Paragraph...
Bullets and Numbering...
Hyperlink...
Synonyms

To move text

1 Select the block of text.

2 Click ✂.

or

3 Open the Edit menu or right-click and select Cut.

4 Place the cursor where you want the text.

5 Click 📋.

or

6 Open the Edit menu or right-click and select Paste.

3

Timesaver tip

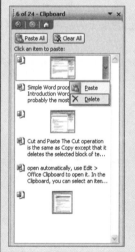

Office XP has its own Clipboard. It can hold 24 items and is controlled through the Task Pane. If the Clipboard does not open automatically, use Edit > Office Clipboard to open it. In the Clipboard, you can select an item to paste or click Paste All to copy all the items at once. The standard Edit > Paste pastes in the last item cut or copied, as normal.

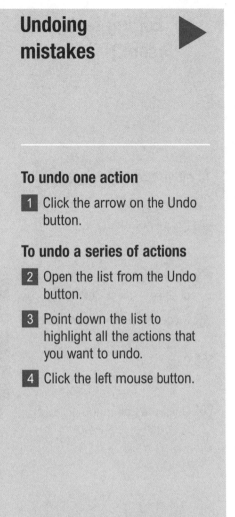

Undoing mistakes ▶

To undo one action

1 Click the arrow on the Undo button.

To undo a series of actions

2 Open the list from the Undo button.

3 Point down the list to highlight all the actions that you want to undo.

4 Click the left mouse button.

Important !

You cannot undo one action from part-way down the list – all those above are also undone.

In the old days, you were lucky if your software allowed you to undo a mistake. With Word, you can go back and undo a whole series of actions. This doesn't just protect you from your mistakes, it also gives you a freedom to experiment. You can do major editing or reformatting, and if at the end you preferred things how they were, you can undo your way back to it. This is managed through the Undo button.

Redo

This is the undo-undo button! If you undid too much, use this to put it back again.

Use it for the last action, or a whole sequence, exactly as with Undo.

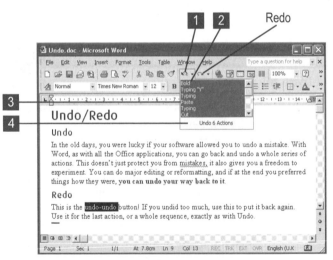

You can add emphasis to text in several ways. The simplest is to make it bold, italic or <u>underlined</u>.

These options can be used by themselves, or in combination – this is **bold and *italic*** – to pick out words within a paragraph, to emphasis whole paragraphs or to make headings stand out more.

You can set these options using the buttons on the Formatting toolbar, the Font dialogue box or the keystroke shortcuts.

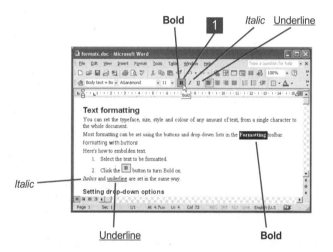

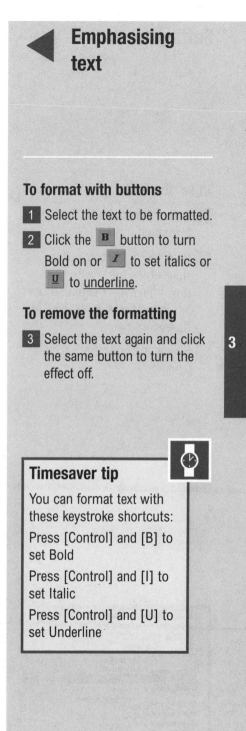

To format with buttons

1 Select the text to be formatted.

2 Click the **B** button to turn Bold on or *I* to set italics or <u>U</u> to <u>underline</u>.

To remove the formatting

3 Select the text again and click the same button to turn the effect off.

3

Timesaver tip

You can format text with these keystroke shortcuts:

Press [Control] and [B] to set Bold

Press [Control] and [I] to set Italic

Press [Control] and [U] to set Underline

Setting fonts

To set the font

1. Select the text to be formatted.

2. Click the ⏷ button to the right of the font name to drop down the list – the names are set in their own fonts, so you have examples.

3. Select an option from the list.

A font is a typeface design, identified by name. There are many thousands of fonts around – Windows comes equipped with several dozen, Word will bring in more as will many other applications.

Fonts can be grouped into four overall categories.

Serif fonts have little 'tails' (the serifs) on the end the long strokes. They are usually very 'readable' and so are normally used for large amounts of text. This paragraph is written in Arial Condensed. Other popular serif fonts include Times New Roman, Georgia and Garamond.

Serif   Sans

Sans serif fonts have simpler lines. They are often used for headings, captions, children's books and other places where small amounts of clear text are wanted. This is Arial. Other sans serif fonts include Helvetica and Tahoma.

Display fonts are those where the visual effect is more important than readability. They are mainly used for headings and in advertisements or posters, where maximum impact is needed. Some display fonts are: **Impact**, Remedy, *Calligraphy* and **STENCIL** .

Picture fonts are sets of special characters and images which can be 'typed' into text. They are mainly used for formulae, marking bullet lists or other special effects. Examples include $\alpha\beta\chi\copyright\sum$ (Symbol) and ☎☺✆❶❷→ (Wingdings).

The font can be set from the drop-down lists on the Formatting toolbar.

The size of the font can be set from the drop-down list beside the Font on the Formatting toolbar.

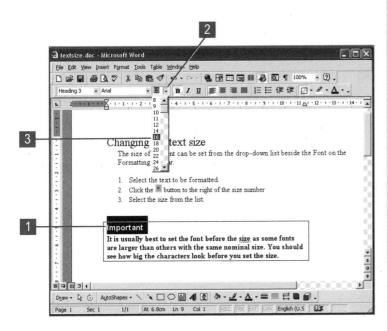

1 Select the text to be formatted.

2 Click the ▾ button to the right of the size number.

3 Select the size from the list.

3

!

Important

It is usually best to set the font before the size as some fonts are larger than others with the same nominal size. You should see how big the characters look before you set the size.

Using the Font dialogue box ▶

If you want to set several font options at the same time – perhaps to make a heading larger, bold and in a different font – or you want to set one of the less-used options, you can do it through the Font dialogue box.

1 Select the text to be formatted.

2 Open the Format menu and select Font…

3 At the Font dialogue box, make sure that you are on the Font tab.

4 Set the font, style, size and/or other options as required.

5 Check the Preview and adjust the settings if necessary.

6 Click OK.

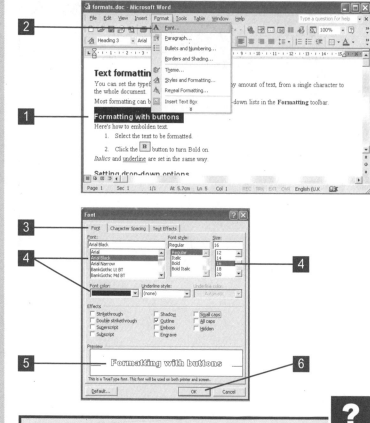

Did you know?

Text size is normally measured in points. This text is 12 point. It can be any size, though you do not usually see it under 6 point or over 72 point in books or magazines.

6 point

9 point

12 point

24 point

48 point

Word offers you two ways to colour text. You can set the font colour – the ink, as it were – or highlight the text by colouring the 'paper' behind it. There are two differences between using text colour and using highlights:

- With highlights you have a smaller choice of colours.
- The Highlight tool can be turned on so that you go through a piece highlighting lots of different words and phrases without having to reselect the tool every time.

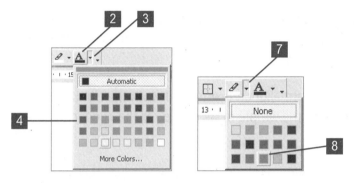

To turn on the highlighter

9 Do not select text, if any is selected already, deselect it by clicking once anywhere on the document.

10 Open the Highlight palette and pick a colour.

11 The cursor will now have a little highlighter icon next to the I beam. Drag the highlighter over the text to be coloured. Repeat as required.

12 To return to normal editing, click once on the Highlight button.

Colouring your text

To set the Font colour

1 Select the text.

2 Click the Font colour button to apply the current colour.

or

3 Click ▾ beside the Font colour button.

4 Pick a colour from the palette.

To highlight text

5 Select the text.

6 Click the Highlight button to apply the current highlight colour.

or

7 Click ▾ beside the Highlight button.

8 Pick a colour from the palette.

3

Aligning text

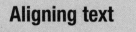

1 Select the paragraph(s) to be formatted. To select a single paragraph, click anywhere inside it. To select several paragraphs in a block, click anywhere inside the first, then drag the highlight down to anywhere in the last.

2 Click the appropriate toolbar button.

Timesaver tip

You can also use these keystroke shortcuts

Press [Control] and [L] for Left alignment

Press [Control] and [R] for Right alignment

Press [Control] and [E] for Centre alignment

Press [Control] and [J] for Justified

The alignment settings control the position of text in relation to the margins.

The alignment options can only be applied to whole paragraphs. A paragraph is selected if any part of it is selected or it contains the insertion point.

In Word, the simplest way to set alignment is to use the toolbar buttons.

Left aligned text is flush with the left margin, but ragged on the right-hand side. It is the default in Word. This text is left aligned.

> Right aligned text is flush with the right margin. A common example of its use is for the sender's address on a letter.

Centre alignment sets each line mid-way between the margins. Headings are often centred.

Justified makes the text flush with the margins on both sides. It gives a page a neater look than left alignment, but can produce wide gaps between words.

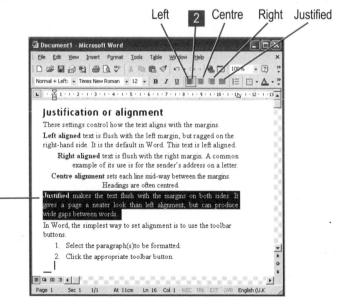

Line spacing

This refers to the amount of vertical space between lines of text. The spacing can only be applied to whole paragraphs and is probably best set through the Paragraph dialogue box.

Text is normally set with single line spacing, so that there is a slim gap between the bottom of one line and the top of the next. This paragraph has single line spacing.

Double spacing is typically used where people want to leave room between the lines for handwritten notes on the printed copy. Publishers used to ask authors to send in their manuscripts double-spaced so that the editor could write corrections on it.

The line spacing can also be set to 1.5 lines or specified in points, a measure used by printers and publishers.

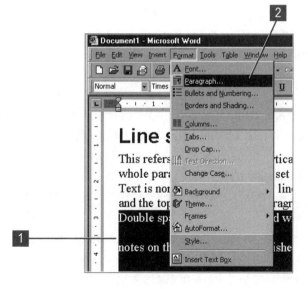

◄ Setting the line spacing

1 Select the paragraph(s).

2 Open the Format menu and select Paragraph...

3 Switch to the Indents and Spacing tab if it is not already on top.

4 Drop down the Line spacing list and select the level.

3

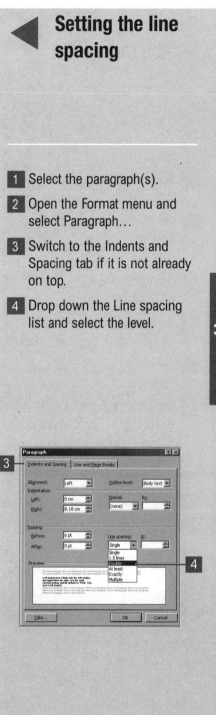

Defining the Page Setup

1. Open the File menu and select Page Setup.

2. On the Margins tab, use the buttons to adjust the margins or enter new values.

3. Set the Orientation – Portrait or Landscape.

4. If required, turn on Mirror margins or 2 pages per sheet.

5. On the Paper tab, pick the Paper size.

6. On the Layout tab, set the Section start and Header and Footer options for large or multi-section documents, if appropriate.

7. Click OK .

If you are creating anything other than routine letters and memos, the Page Setup may well need changing.

Paper size

You will need to change the size if you are printing on envelopes or unusual paper, and should always check it when working from a template, which may have been set up for US paper size. Use this tab also to set the orientation – upright (Portrait) or sideways (Landscape).

Setting margins

Use the Margins tab to adjust the space around the printed area. Margins should not be too small – printers can't reach the very edge of the paper and you need some white space around any text. Sometimes a slight reduction of the margins will give you a better printout. There is little more irritating than a couple of odd lines of text or a tiny block of data on a separate sheet.

If you are printing both sides of the paper, book-style, tick the Mirror margins box. If they are to be ring-bound, widen the inner margin or set the gutter (the space inside the inner margin) to allow for the hidden paper.

Paper source

This rarely needs attention. You might perhaps want to turn off the defaults so that you can manually feed in individual sheets of card or special paper, without emptying the paper tray.

Layout

This needs attention with large documents that have been divided into sections – you can set where each section starts – and where you have headers and footers, and don't want the same ones on every page.

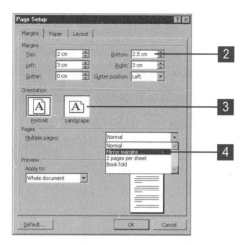

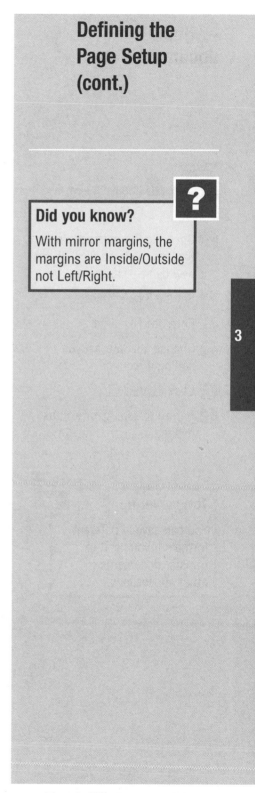

Did you know? ?

With mirror margins, the margins are Inside/Outside not Left/Right.

3

Saving a document

There are two file-saving routines in Word, as in most Windows applications.

- Save is used to save an existing file after editing – just click 🖫 or open the File menu and select Save.
- Save As is used to save a new file, or to save an existing file with a new name or in a new folder – see the steps.

1 Click 🖫 to save a new file.

or

2 Open the File menu and select Save As to save a file with a new name or location.

3 Set the Save in folder.

4 Enter the Filename.

5 Change the Save as type setting if required.

6 Click ▭ Save ▭.

7 Return to editing, or exit, as desired.

Timesaver tip

You can save in different formats if you need to transfer documents to other applications.

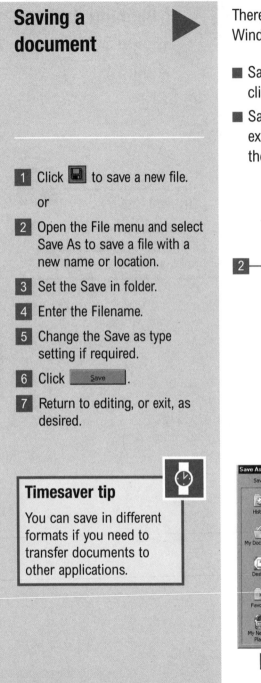

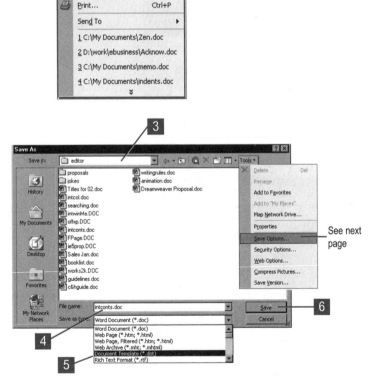

See next page

Save options

If you select General Options from the Tools drop-down list on the Save dialogue box, it opens an extensive Options panel in Word. The key options are those which protect the file:

- Password to open, prevents all unauthorised access.
- Password to modify allows anyone to read it, but only the password holder can save it, with the same name.
- Read recommended sets Read Only as the default mode for opening the file.
- If you have any doubts about the PC's reliability, turn on Always create Backup copy.
- Save AutoRecover guards against lost work – set a reasonable interval.

If you have any doubts about the PC's reliability, turn on Always create Backup copy

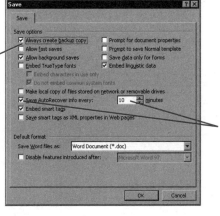

Save AutoRecover guards against lost work – set a reasonable interval

! Important

When you Save As in Word, a filename is created for you from the first line of the document. If it is not suitable, replace it with your own.

Printing a document

Word is WYSIWYG (What You See Is What You Get), so that what you see on screen is very close to its appearance when printed. Because of this, using the Print button 🖨 on the Standard toolbar works well most of the time. If you want to print selected pages, or need several copies, or have other special requirements, the Print dialoguebox gives you more control of the output.

To control the printing

1 If you only want to print part of a page, select the text first.

2 Open the File menu and select Print.

3 Set the range of pages to print.

4 Set the Copies number – turn on Collate to print multiple copies in sorted sets.

5 For double-sided printing, set the Print option to Odd pages, then feed the paper back in – in reverse order – and repeat with Even pages.

6 Click OK.

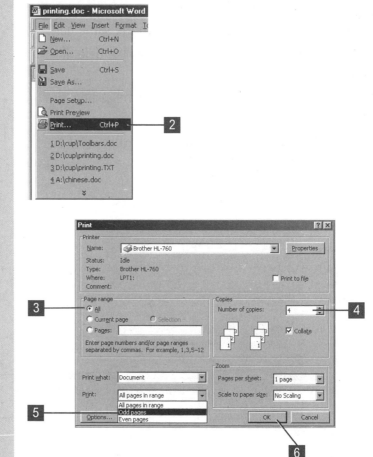

Important !

If you select text before starting, the Selection option will be available in the Page Range area.

Timesaver tip

To print one copy of the whole document, using the default printer, just click 🖨.

If you work in Print Layout view, you can see – as you create the document – how it will fit on paper. By dropping the Zoom level down to Whole page or Two pages, you can get a better impression of the overall layout of the document.

Print Preview lets you view more pages – as thumbnails – at a time, has a Zoom tool which you can use to jump between 100% and the preview size, and shows the headers and footers more clearly. When previewing, you can still adjust font sizes, line spacing or the size and position of objects to get a better balanced page – all the normal menu commands are available and toolbars can be opened as needed.

3

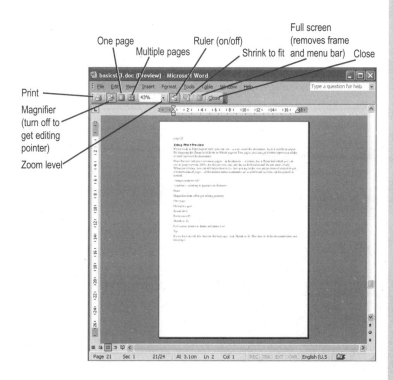

One page
Multiple pages
Ruler (on/off)
Shrink to fit
Full screen (removes frame and menu bar)
Close

Print
Magnifier (turn off to get editing pointer)
Zoom level

Timesaver tip

If you have an odd few lines on the last page, click Shrink to fit. This tries to fit the document onto one less page.

Getting Help

1. If the Assistant is not visible, click 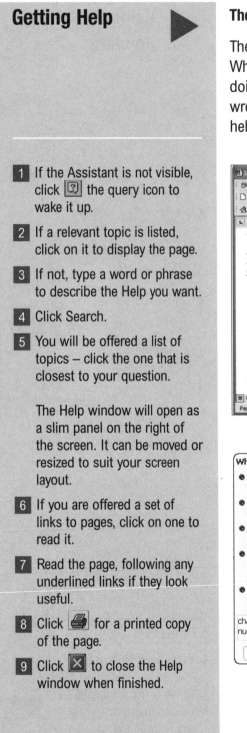 the query icon to wake it up.

2. If a relevant topic is listed, click on it to display the page.

3. If not, type a word or phrase to describe the Help you want.

4. Click Search.

5. You will be offered a list of topics – click the one that is closest to your question.

   The Help window will open as a slim panel on the right of the screen. It can be moved or resized to suit your screen layout.

6. If you are offered a set of links to pages, click on one to read it.

7. Read the page, following any underlined links if they look useful.

8. Click 🖶 for a printed copy of the page.

9. Click ❌ to close the Help window when finished.

The Office Assistant

The Assistant is a friendly way into the Help system. When you call on it for help, it will look at what you are doing and offer you some likely topics. If it guesses wrong – as it often does – then just tell it what you need help with, and it will provide the answer.

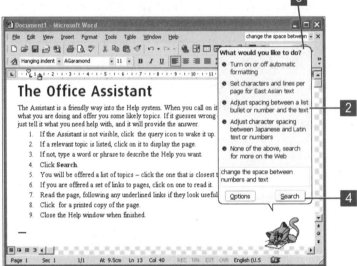

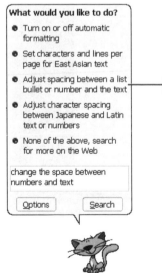

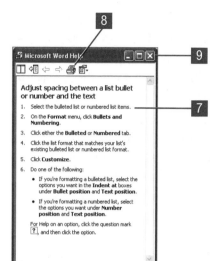

8

9

7

Microsoft Word Help

Adjust spacing between a list bullet or number and the text

1. Select the bulleted list or numbered list items.

2. On the **Format** menu, click **Bullets and Numbering**.

3. Click either the **Bulleted** or **Numbered** tab.

4. Click the list format that matches your list's existing bulleted list or numbered list format.

5. Click **Customize**.

6. Do one of the following:

   • If you're formatting a bulleted list, select the options you want in the **Indent at** boxes under **Bullet position** and **Text position**.

   • If you're formatting a numbered list, select the options you want under **Number position** and **Text position**.

   For Help on an option, click the question mark ?, and then click the option.

Getting Help (cont.)

3

Did you know?

You can choose the appearance of the Assistant. Right-click on it, select Choose Assistant… from the short menu and see which you prefer.

You do not have to use the Assistant – you can get into the Help system from the Help menu. If you do not want to use it, right-click on the Assistant and select Hide from the short menu.

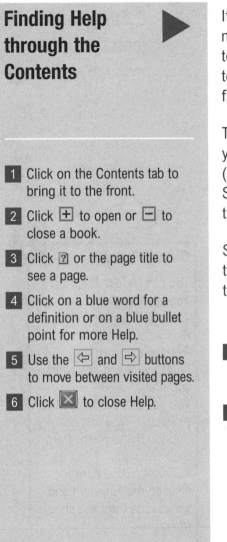

Finding Help through the Contents ▶

1. Click on the Contents tab to bring it to the front.

2. Click ⊞ to open or ⊟ to close a book.

3. Click ? or the page title to see a page.

4. Click on a blue word for a definition or on a blue bullet point for more Help.

5. Use the ⇦ and ⇨ buttons to move between visited pages.

6. Click ☒ to close Help.

If you use the Office Assistant to access the Help, all you normally see are the pages of Help text, but there is more to Help. Click ⊲ the Show button, on the left of the toolbar, and a panel opens. Its tabs give you three ways to find Help.

The most useful of these is the Contents tab, from which you can browse through the Help pages. Pick a heading (with a ◆ icon) and open that to see the page titles. Some sections have subsections, making it a two or three-stage process to get to page titles.

Some Help topics are stand-alone pages; some have a top page with a set of links to pages on different parts of the topic.

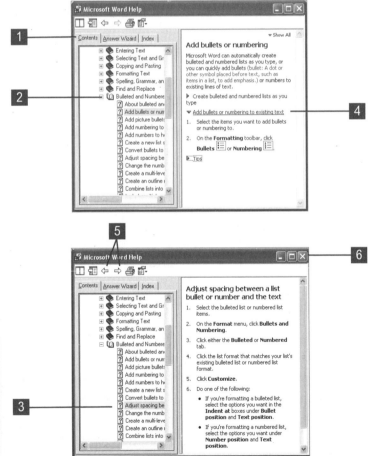

If you want to search through all the possible references, try the Index. A search here will find every page on which the search word occurs. A single word may give you too many results – focus on the pages you want by giving two or more search words.

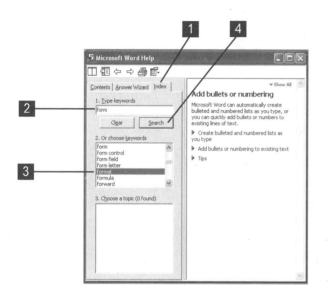

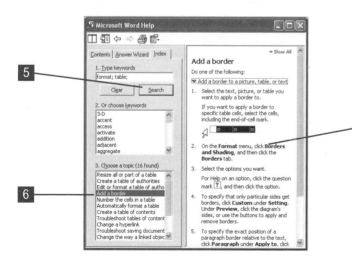

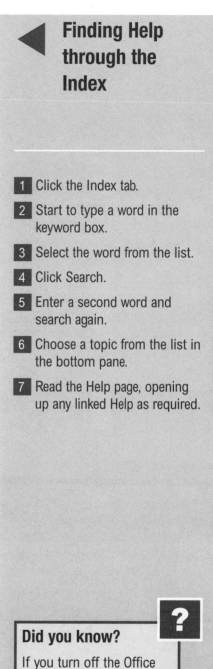

Finding Help through the Index

1 Click the Index tab.

2 Start to type a word in the keyword box.

3 Select the word from the list.

4 Click Search.

5 Enter a second word and search again.

6 Choose a topic from the list in the bottom pane.

7 Read the Help page, opening up any linked Help as required.

Did you know?

If you turn off the Office Assistant, you can use the Answer Wizard tab of the Help system to ask questions in exactly the same way.

Managing your files

4

Introduction

To be able to use your computer efficiently, you must know how to manage your files – how to find, copy, move, rename and delete them – and how to organise the folders on your disks. In Windows XP, these jobs can be done through either Windows Explorer or My Computer – the two are almost identical. In this chapter we will have a look at these and see how they can be used for file and folder management. We will also look at creating links between documents and applications, and at the Recycle Bin – a neat device which makes it much less likely that you will delete files by accident.

The hard disk is the main place for storing files, but it is not the only one. Files can also be written on floppy disks and CD-ROM disks, for backup storage, or to move from one PC to another. We will be looking at these external storage media towards the end of the chapter.

Understanding files and folders

The hard disks supplied on modern PCs are typically 20 gigabytes or larger. 1 Gigabyte is 1 billion bytes and each byte can hold one character (or part of a number or of a graphic). That means that a typical hard disk can store nearly 4 billion words – enough for about 20,000 hefty novels! More to the point, if you were using it to store letters and reports, it could hold many, many thousands of them. Even if you are storing big audio or video files you are still going to get hundreds of them on the disk. It must be organised if you are ever to find your files.

Folders

Folders provide this organisation. They are containers in which related files can be placed to keep them together, and away from other files. A folder can also contain sub-folders – which can themselves by subdivided. You can think of the first level of folders as being sets of filing cabinets; those at the second level are drawers within the cabinets, and the next level are equivalent to divisions within the drawers. (And these could have subdividers – there is no limit to this.)

You can just store all your files in My Documents, but it will get terribly crowded! Have a separate folder for each type of file, or each area of work, subdividing as necessary, so that no folder holds more than a few dozen files.

Paths

The structure of folders is often referred to as the tree. It starts at the root, which is the drive letter – C: for your main hard disk – and branches off from there.

A folder's position in the tree is described by its path. For most operations, you can identify a folder by clicking on it in a screen display, but now and then you will have to type its path. This should start at the drive letter and the root, and include every folder along the branch, with a backslash (\) between the names.

For example:

    C:\DTP
    C:\WordProcessing\Letters2006

When you want to know a path, look it up in the Explorer display and trace the branches down from the root.

Filenames

A filename has two parts – the name and an extension.

The name can be as long as you like, and include almost any characters – including spaces. But don't let this freedom go to your head. The longer the name, the greater the opportunity for typing errors. The most important thing to remember when naming a file is that the name must mean something to you, so that you can find it easily next time you want to use it.

The extension can be from 0 to 3 characters, and is separated from the rest of the name by a dot. It is used to identify the nature of the file. Windows uses the extensions COM, EXE, SYS, INI, DLL to identify special files of its own – handle these with care!

Most applications also use their own special extensions. Word-processor files are often marked with DOC; spreadsheet files are usually XLS; database files typically have DB extensions.

If you are saving a file in a word-processor, spreadsheet or other application, and are asked for a filename, you normally only have to give the first part. The application will take care of the extension. If you do need to give an extension, make it meaningful. BAK is a good extension for backup files; TXT for text files.

When an application asks you for a filename – and the file is in the *current* folder – type in the name and extension only. If the file is in *another* folder, type in the path, a backslash separator and then the filename.

For example:

    MYFILE.DOC
    C:\WORPROC\REPORTS\MAY25.TXT
    A:\MYFILE.BAK

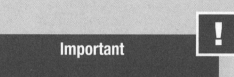

Important

If there are several users, they will each have their own 'My Documents' folder set up by Windows XP – any new folders should be created within this.

4

A PC will have one or more hard drives, plus a floppy disk drive and a CD-ROM drive, all of which can be used for storing files. 'My Documents' and 'Shared Documents' are actually on the C: hard drive, but Windows creates several routes to these and to other much-used folders. If you replace the Tasks panel on the left, with the Folders display (and you will see how to do that shortly), then there are more direct links to different parts of the system.

Browsing for files

▶

Don't worry overmuch about remembering paths. When you want to access a file in an application, you will usually be taken to an Open dialogue box in which you can select the drive, folder and file from a graphical display. Those that do not open this dialogue box directly will have a button to open it.

Browsing dialogue boxes from two applications.

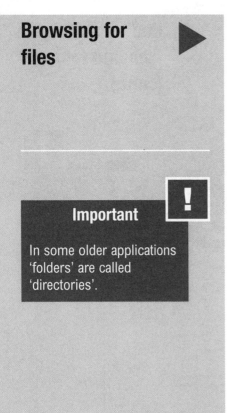

Important

In some older applications 'folders' are called 'directories'.

Jargon buster

Root – the folder of the disk. All other folders branch off from the root.
Parent – a folder that contains another.
Child – a sub-folder of a Parent.
Branch – the structure of sub-folders open off from a folder.

Windows Explorer is the main application for finding and managing your files.

In the Explorer window, the main working area is split, with folders in the Explorer Bar, and the contents on the right.

The Folder List may show the disk drives and first level of folders only, but folders can be expanded to show the sub-folders.

The Contents shows the files and sub-folders in the currently selected folder. These can be displayed as thumbnails, tiles, icons or with details of the file's size, type and date it was last modified.

The Status Bar shows information about the selected file(s) or folders.

The Toolbar has the buttons for the most commonly-used commands. Others can be added, if desired.

The Explorer Bar can also be used to display Common Tasks, Search, Favorites or History, as well as Folders.

Exploring Windows Explorer

To start Explorer

1 Click ⟨ start ⟩ .

2 Point to All Programs then to Accessories.

3 Click Windows Explorer.

4 Click on a folder's icon or its name to open it and display its contents.

4

Explorer bar, displaying the Folder List

Current folder

First level folder

Sub-folder

Status Bar

Contents – here shown in Icon View

Exploring My Computer ▶

My Computer is actually the same program as Windows Explorer, but it looks rather different. This is because when it first starts, it focuses on a different part of the system, and it has different display settings. Any or all of these can be changed.

The Standard toolbar buttons

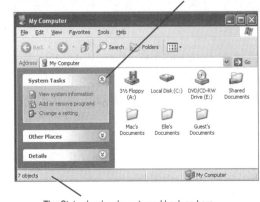

Click to expand/collapse the display of items

The Status bar has been turned back on here

⬅ Back ▾	Go back to previous folder
➡ ▾	Go to next folder
🔼	Go to parent folder
🔍 Search	Search for files
📂 Folders	Switch between Folder List and Common Tasks in the panel on the left
▦ ▾	Alternative views of files

Use the drop-down list to switch to drives or folders higher up the same path

My Computer
- My Documents
- My Computer
  - 3½ Floppy (A:)
  - Local Disk (C:)
  - DVD/CD-RW Drive (E:)
  - Control Panel
  - Shared Documents
  - Mac's Documents
  - Elle's Documents
  - Guest's Documents
  - My Network Places
  - Recycle Bin
  - My Briefcase

Timesaver tip

Remember that My Computer and Windows Explorer are the same program and can be used and customised in the same ways.

The display options can be set from the View menu and the Views button. These options can be set at any time, and can be different for different folders. There are two areas of choice: which of the toolbars and other control bars are to be open; how files and folders are displayed.

Toolbars

- The Standard is pretty well essential.
- The Address is useful. Its drop-down outline of the folder structure offers a quick way to move between drives.
- The Links carries quick links to selected websites.

The Address and Links toolbars are more useful when you have turned Windows Explorer into Internet Explorer and are using it to explore the web (see Chapter 9).

(see Chapter 9)

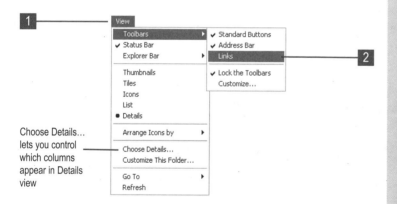

Choose Details...
lets you control
which columns
appear in Details
view

To display Toolbars

1 Open the View menu.

2 Point to Toolbars then click on a toolbar to turn it on or off.

4

Displaying the Explorer toolbars (cont.)

Common file icons

	Bitmap image
	GIF image
	Web page
	Text
	Word document
	Excel workbook
	Open Type font
	System file – handle with care!

The contents of the Standard toolbar are not fixed. You can add or remove buttons, move them around within the bar, and adjust their appearance. This is all done through the Customise Toolbar dialogue box.

There are buttons available for most of the other commands in the menus, including Cut, Copy, Paste, Copy To Folder and Move To Folder (all from the Edit menu) which can be used for copying and moving files and folders, instead of dragging.

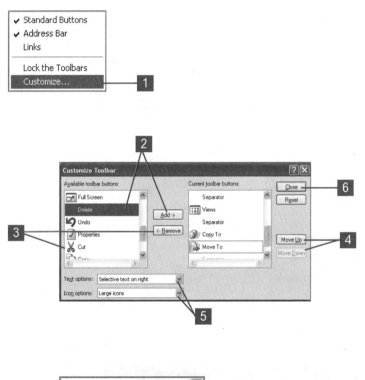

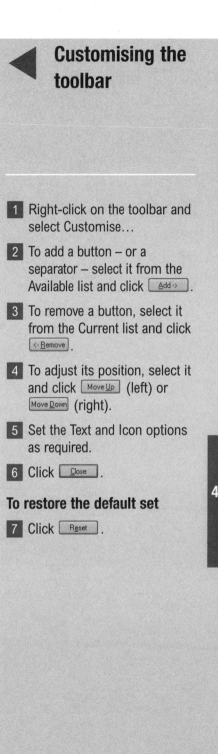

1. Right-click on the toolbar and select Customise...

2. To add a button – or a separator – select it from the Available list and click ⌊ Add ⌋.

3. To remove a button, select it from the Current list and click ⌊ <- Remove ⌋.

4. To adjust its position, select it and click ⌊ Move Up ⌋ (left) or ⌊Move Down⌋ (right).

5. Set the Text and Icon options as required.

6. Click ⌊ Close ⌋.

To restore the default set

7. Click ⌊ Reset ⌋.

4

Viewing files

1 Open the View menu.

   or

2 Click 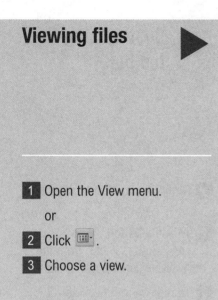.

3 Choose a view.

Filmstrip is only available in folders that have been customised for pictures. It shows a large image of the selected file, with the rest in a strip across the bottom.

Thumbnails show little previews of files, if possible. Graphics and Web pages will be displayed, and Word, PowerPoint and Excel documents will display if they were saved with a preview.

Tiles shows a large, easy to recognise icon, accompanied by key details of the file.

Icons and List show lots of files in little space.

Details shows the name, type, size and date of files. The display can be sorted by any of these.

Icons view

Tiles view

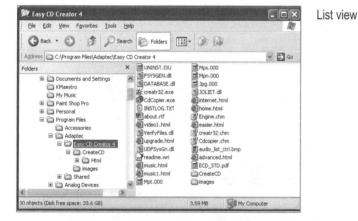

List view

Details view

4

Viewing files (cont.)

Filmstrip view

Thumbnails view

The Folders structure can be shown in outline form, or with some or all of its branches shown in full. The best display is always the simplest one that will show you all you need. This usually means that most of the structure is collapsed back to its first level of main folders, with one or two branches expanded to show particular sub-folders. It is sometimes worth expanding the whole lot, just to get an idea of the overall structure and to see how sub-folders fit together.

If a folder has sub-folders, it will have a symbol beside it.

+ has sub-folders, and can be expanded

– sub-folders displayed and can be collapsed.

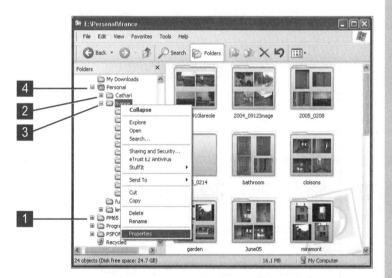

To expand a folder

1 Click + by its name.

2 Click + by any sub-folders if you want to fully expand the whole branching set.

To collapse a folder

3 Click – by its name.

To collapse a whole branch

4 Click – by the folder at the top of the branched set.

4

Setting the folder type ▶

Windows can be set to handle folders in slightly different ways if they hold pictures, sound or video files. This will affect the Tasks display – unless you have replaced these by Folders – and the default View setting.

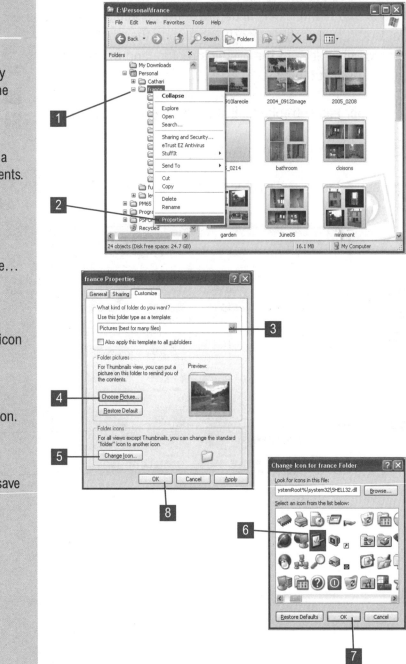

1 In Windows Explorer or My Computer, right-click on the folder.

2 Select Properties.

3 On the Customise tab pick a folder type to suit the contents.

Change the picture

4 If you want to change the image on the front of the folder, click Choose Picture… and browse for one.

Change the icon

5 If you want to change the icon used for the folder by Windows Explorer, click Change Icon…

6 Select the most suitable icon.

7 Click OK.

8 Back at the Properties dialogue box, click OK to save your settings.

These control the overall appearance of folders and the way that files are handled. The dialogue box has four tabs.

On the General tab there are three options:

- Select 'Show common tasks in folders' to enable them – the actual display is toggled by the Folders button.
- You can open each folder in a new or in the same window.
- You can select items with a single or double-click.

The View panel controls the display of files. There are two main options here. The first is whether to show 'hidden' files. These are mainly found in the Windows and Windows/System folders. They are ones that you do not usually need to see and which are safer out of the way.

- Application extensions – files with .DLL extensions. They are used by applications and must not be deleted.
- System files – marked by .SYS after the name. These are essential to Windows' internal workings.
- Drivers – with .VXD or .DRV extensions. These make printers, screens and other hardware work properly.

The second key choice is whether you want to set different display styles for different folders – turn on 'Remember each folder's view settings' if you do. If you have a mixture of styles already and want all folders to look the same, you can use the buttons to make them all look like the current folder or reset them all to their default settings.

The File Types tab is used to link programs and documents.

The Offline Files tab is for use where files are stored on a network. The tab's options are not normally active on a single PC.

4

Setting Folder Options (cont.)

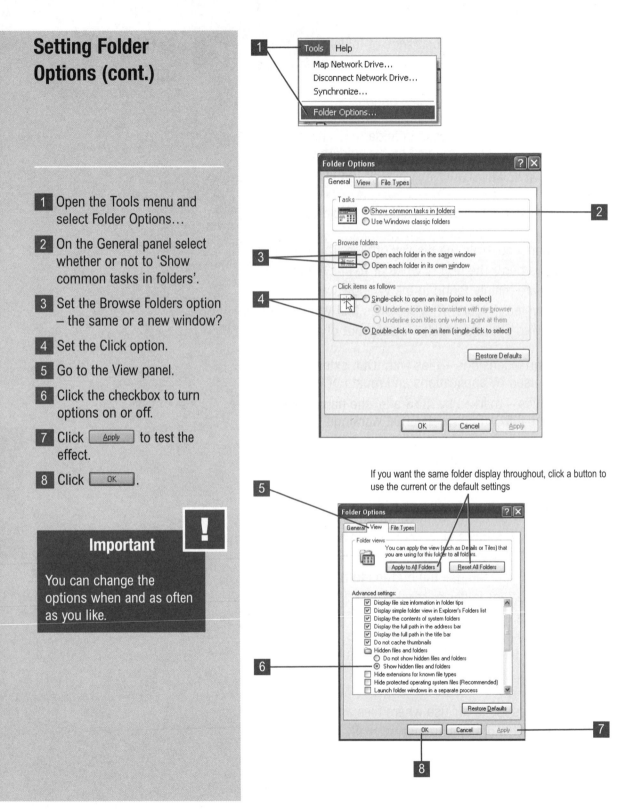

1. Open the Tools menu and select Folder Options...

2. On the General panel select whether or not to 'Show common tasks in folders'.

3. Set the Browse Folders option – the same or a new window?

4. Set the Click option.

5. Go to the View panel.

6. Click the checkbox to turn options on or off.

7. Click Apply to test the effect.

8. Click OK.

Important !

You can change the options when and as often as you like.

If you want the same folder display throughout, click a button to use the current or the default settings

Windows keeps a list of registered file types. These are ones that it knows how to handle. If you open a document of a known type, the system will run the appropriate application and load in the file. There are some types that Windows doesn't know about and others which you may prefer to open with a different program. The associations are easily made or changed through the File Types tab of the Folder Options dialogue box.

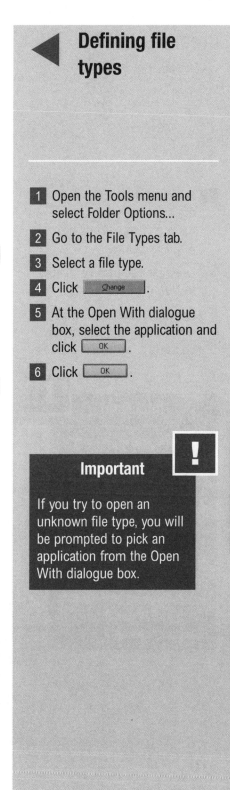

Defining file types

1 Open the Tools menu and select Folder Options...

2 Go to the File Types tab.

3 Select a file type.

4 Click   Change .

5 At the Open With dialogue box, select the application and click   OK .

6 Click   OK .

Important

4

If you try to open an unknown file type, you will be prompted to pick an application from the Open With dialogue box.

Creating a folder ▶

Organised people set up their folders before they need them, so that they have places to store their letters – private and business, reports, memos, notes, and whatever, when they start to write them on their new system. They have a clear idea of the structure that they want, and create their folders at the right branches.

1 Select the folder that will be the parent of your new one, or the root if you want a new first-level folder.

2 Open the File menu and point to New then select Folder.

3 Replace 'New Folder' with a new name – any length, any characters, as with filenames.

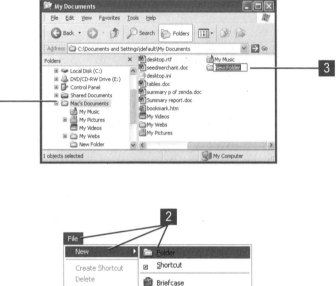

Timesaver tip

If you want to change the name of a folder, right-click on it and select Rename, or use 'Rename this folder' from the Common Tasks display.

Organised people may set up their folders before they create the documents that will go into them, but the rest of us set up our new folders when the old ones get so full that it is difficult to find things. Nor do we always create them in the most suitable place in the tree. Fortunately, Windows XP caters for us too. Files can easily be moved from one folder to another, and folders can easily be moved to new places on the tree.

Here, Web pix is being moved from within my Work folder into Shared Pictures, so that others can access it.

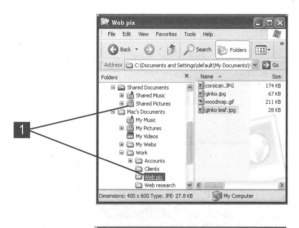

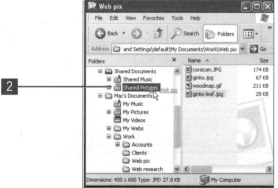

Timesaver tip

Copying a folder – and all its files – to another disk can be a quick way to make a backup of a set of files.

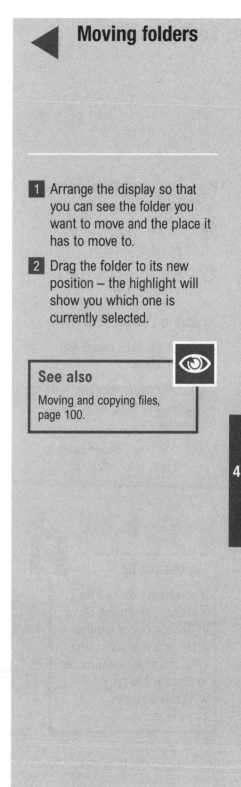

Moving folders

1 Arrange the display so that you can see the folder you want to move and the place it has to move to.

2 Drag the folder to its new position – the highlight will show you which one is currently selected.

See also

Moving and copying files, page 100.

4

Sorting files

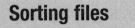

Unless you specify otherwise, folders and files are listed in alphabetical order. Most of the time this works fine, but when you are moving or copying files, or hunting for them, other arrangements can be more convenient. You can sort them into order of name, type, size or the Date that they were last used.

If you are using Details View, sorting is very easy to do

1 Open the View menu and point to Arrange Icons By.

2 Select Name, Size, Type, or Modified (date).

To sort in Details View

3 Open the View menu and select Details.

4 To sort by Name, Size, Type or Date, click on the column header.

5 Click on the header again to sort into reverse order.

Timesaver tip

If you have a lot of files in a folder, turn on the Show in Groups option on the Arrange Icons sub-menu. This can make them easier to handle. The option works in all Views, except List.

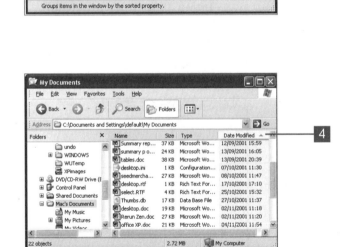

The amount of information in a My Computer or Windows Explorer display can vary greatly, depending upon the number of items in a folder and the display style. You should be able to adjust the display so that you can see things properly.

As well as being able to set the overall size of the window, you can also adjust the width of each field in a Details display, and the split between the Folders and Contents panes of Explorer.

To adjust the columns

1 Point the cursor at the dividing line between two field headings.

2 When the cursor changes to ↔, drag the dividing line to change the width of the field on its left.

To move the window divider

3 Point anywhere on the bar between the panes to get the ↔ cursor.

4 Drag the shadowed line to adjust the relative size of the panes.

4

Selecting files ▶

You can easily select one file by clicking on it, but you can also select sets of files. This is useful when you want to back up a day's work by copying the new files to a floppy, or move a set from one folder to another or delete a load of unwanted files.

You can select:

- a block of adjacent files
- a scattered set
- the whole folder-full.

The same techniques work with all display styles.

To select a block using the mouse

1 Point to one corner of the block and click.

2 Drag an outline onto the ones you want.

To [Shift] select

3 Click on the file at one end of the block.

4 If necessary, scroll the window to bring the other end into view.

5 Hold [Shift].

6 Click on the far end file.

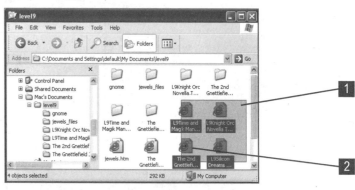

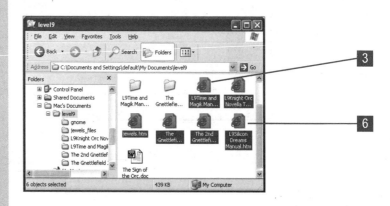

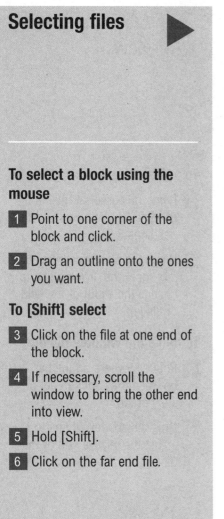

Timesaver tip

It may be easier to arrange icons by Name, Date or Type, before you start to select.

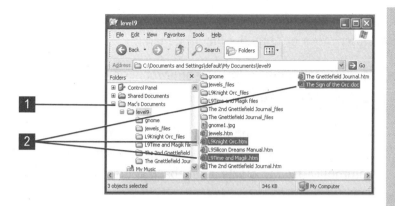

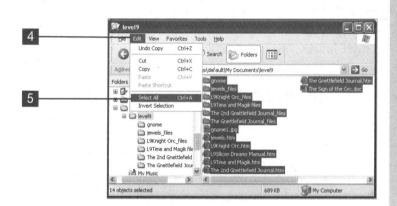

To select scattered files

1 Click on any one of the files you want.

2 Hold [Control] and click each of the other files.

3 You can deselect any file by clicking on it a second time.

To select all the files

4 Open the Edit menu.

5 Choose Select All.

Timesaver tip

If you want all the files except for a scattered few, select those few, then use Edit > Invert Selection to deselect them and select the others.

Moving and copying files

▶

1. Select the file(s).
2. Scroll the Folders list so that you can see the target folder – don't click on it!
3. Point to any one of the selected files and drag to the target.

   or

4. Hold down the right mouse button while you drag then select Move or Copy.

Timesaver tip

The easiest way to copy a file to a floppy is to right-click on it to open its context menu, then point to Send To and select the floppy drive.

When you drag a file from one place to another, it will either move or copy the file. In general:

- It is a move if you drag to somewhere on the same disk.
- It is a copy if you drag the file to a different disk.

When you are dragging files within a disk, you are usually moving to reorganise your storage; and copying is most commonly used to create a safe backup on a separate disk.

If you want to move a file from one disk to another, or copy within a disk, hold down the right mouse button while you drag. A menu will appear when you reach the target folder. You can select Move or Copy from there.

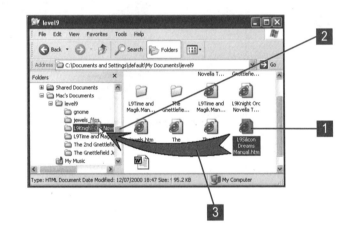

Move To Folder/Copy To Folder

If you are having difficulty arranging the Explorer display so that you can see the source files and the target folder, the simplest approach is to use the Move To Folder or Copy To Folder commands. These let you pick the target folder through a dialogue box.

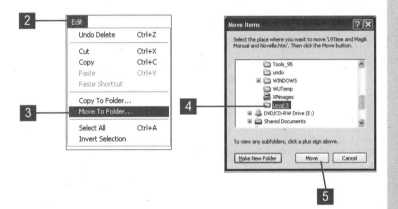

1. Select the file(s).
2. Open the Edit menu.
3. Select Copy To or Move To Folder.
4. Select the target drive or folder.
5. Click Move or Copy.

Timesaver tip

You can use the Cut, Copy and Paste commands to move and copy files and folders. Find them on the Edit menu, or on the context menu when you right-click on a file or in a folder.

Copy stores a copy of the file or folder in the Clipboard.

Cut removes the original file, storing a copy in the Clipboard.

Paste puts a copy of the stored file into the current folder.

4

Renaming files ▶

You can rename a file if necessary – and it may well be necessary if the original name was created automatically by a program, as happens when you import images from a digital camera into the PC.

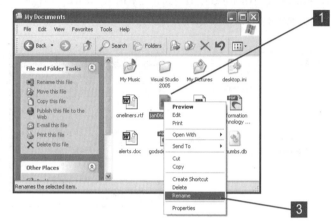

1. Select the file.
2. Press [F2] on your keyboard.

   or

3. Open the File menu or the right-click menu and select Rename.
4. Edit the name as required and press [Enter] to fix the new name.

In the earlier days of computing, it was all too easy to delete a file by mistake, wiping out hours or days – or even weeks – of work. Windows protects you from yourself! When you delete a file, it is not immediately erased from the hard disk. Instead it is taken from its folder and placed in the Recycle Bin, from which it can easily be recovered.

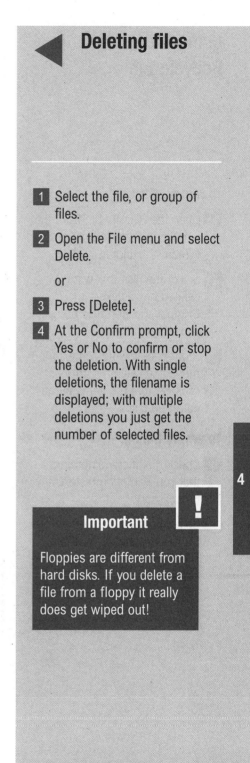

Confirm Multiple File Delete

Are you sure you want to send these 3 items to the Recycle Bin?

[Yes]   [No]

4

Deleting files

1 Select the file, or group of files.

2 Open the File menu and select Delete.

or

3 Press [Delete].

4 At the Confirm prompt, click Yes or No to confirm or stop the deletion. With single deletions, the filename is displayed; with multiple deletions you just get the number of selected files.

4

Important

Floppies are different from hard disks. If you delete a file from a floppy it really does get wiped out!

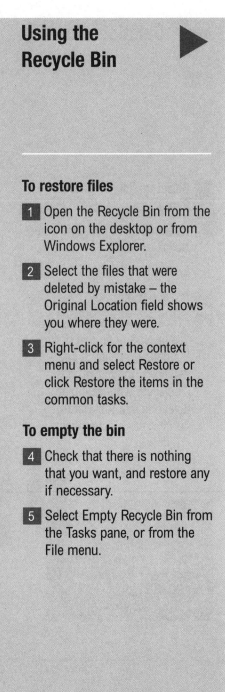

Using the Recycle Bin

To restore files

1. Open the Recycle Bin from the icon on the desktop or from Windows Explorer.

2. Select the files that were deleted by mistake – the Original Location field shows you where they were.

3. Right-click for the context menu and select Restore or click Restore the items in the common tasks.

To empty the bin

4. Check that there is nothing that you want, and restore any if necessary.

5. Select Empty Recycle Bin from the Tasks pane, or from the File menu.

This is a wonderful feature, especially for those of us given to making instant decisions that we later regret. Until you empty the Bin, any 'deleted' files and folders can be instantly restored – and if the folder that they were stored in has also been deleted, that is re-created first, so things go back into their proper place.

Files sent to the Recycle Bin stay there until you empty it. Do this regularly, to free up disk space.

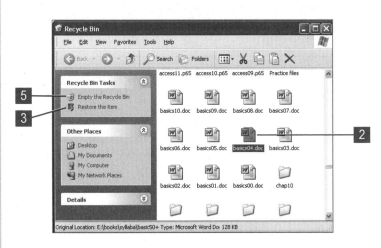

Timesaver tip

You can delete folders or files by dragging them directly to the Recycle Bin.

This is not something you will do every day, for deleting a folder also deletes its files, and files are usually precious things. But we all acquire programs we don't need, keep files long past their use-by dates, and sometimes create unnecessary folders.

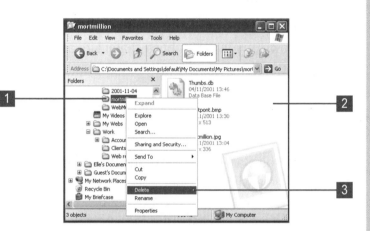

◀ **Deleting folders**

1 Select the folder.

2 Check the files list. Are there any there? Do you want any of them? No, then carry on.

3 Right-click on the folder to open the context menu or open the File menu and select Delete.

4 If necessary, you can stop the process by clicking No when you are asked to confirm that the folder is to be thrown in the Bin.

! 4

Important

If you delete a folder by mistake it can be restored from the Recycle Bin.

Finding files

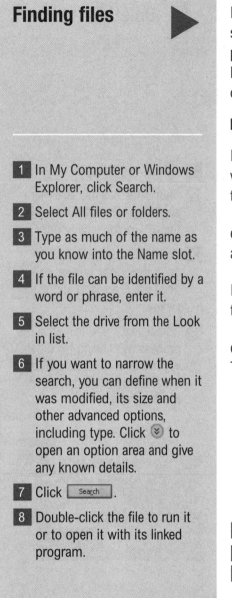

1. In My Computer or Windows Explorer, click Search.

2. Select All files or folders.

3. Type as much of the name as you know into the Name slot.

4. If the file can be identified by a word or phrase, enter it.

5. Select the drive from the Look in list.

6. If you want to narrow the search, you can define when it was modified, its size and other advanced options, including type. Click ✷ to open an option area and give any known details.

7. Click [Search].

8. Double-click the file to run it or to open it with its linked program.

If you are well organised, have a clear and logical structure of folders and consistently store files in their proper places, you should rarely need this facility. However, if you are like me, you will be grateful for it. You can find files by name, type, age, size or contents.

Partial names and wildcards

If you type part of a name into the name box, the Search will track down any file with those characters anywhere in the name.

e.g. 'DOC' will find 'My Documents', 'Letter to doctor', and all Word files with a .DOC extension.

If you know the start of the name and the extension, fill the gap with the wildcard*. (include the dot!)

e.g. *REP*.TXT* will find 'REPORT MAY 15.*TXT*', 'REPLY TO IRS.TXT' and similar files.

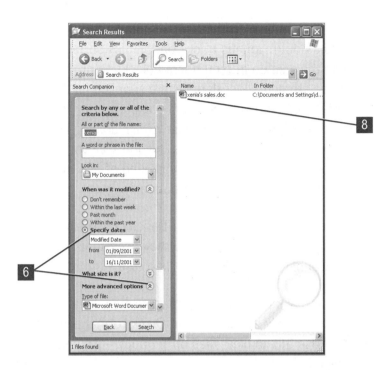

6

8

Timesaver tip

You can also begin by
selecting Search on the
Start menu.

4

Timesaver tip

Working from within the
Search window, you can
print, delete and otherwise
manage a found file
through the options on the
File menu.

Formatting a floppy ▶

1 Insert the disk into the drive.

2 Run My Computer or Windows Explorer.

3 Right-click on the A: drive icon and

4 Select Format.

5 Make sure that it is set for the right Capacity.

6 Set a Format option if wanted.

7 Click [OK].

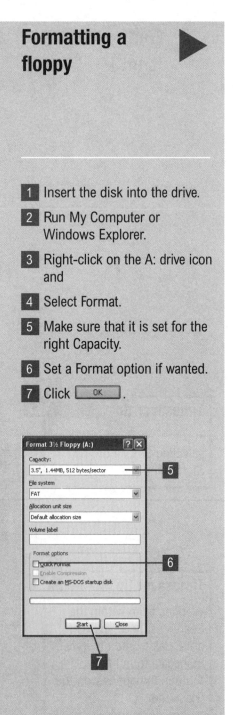

Before a floppy disk can be used it must be formatted. This marks out magnetic tracks on the disk surface, dividing the area up into numbered blocks to provide organised storage. Most floppies are supplied ready-formatted, but some are not. And sometimes formatting an old disk will give it a new lease of life, erasing any old data. The Format command does this job – all you have to do is make sure that you know what kind of disk you are formatting, and possibly set an option.

PC disks are almost always High-Density (HD) standard – 3.5 inch, 1.44Mb capacities. You may occasionally meet a 720Kb Double-Density (DD) 3.5 inch disk.

Most new disks are now sold pre-formatted, so a full format may rarely be needed, but Quick Format is very handy – use this to clear files off a floppy – it's faster than deleting them!

CDs come in three varieties

A CD-ROM is read-only memory. You can read data from this kind of CD, but you cannot write it onto it. Applications software is normally supplied on CD-ROM nowadays.

A CD-W disk is writeable – you can store data on it. But this is a one-off thing. Once you have written data onto it, you cannot change what is stored there, or add more data.

A CD-R disk is rewriteable – you can store data on it, but you can add more data later, or update the files stored there. The only limitation is this. Writing really is a once-only process – it changes the surface of the disk irredeemably. When you erase something from the disk, or replace a file with a newer copy, you cannot reuse the space which had been occupied by the old file. With reuse, CD-R gradually fills up.

You must have a CD-writer drive, and not a simple CD drive, to be able to do this.

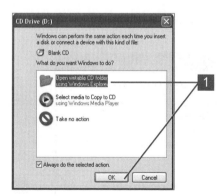

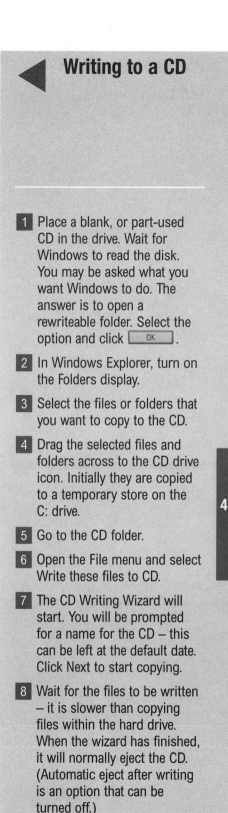

1 Place a blank, or part-used CD in the drive. Wait for Windows to read the disk. You may be asked what you want Windows to do. The answer is to open a rewriteable folder. Select the option and click [OK].

2 In Windows Explorer, turn on the Folders display.

3 Select the files or folders that you want to copy to the CD.

4 Drag the selected files and folders across to the CD drive icon. Initially they are copied to a temporary store on the C: drive.

5 Go to the CD folder.

6 Open the File menu and select Write these files to CD.

7 The CD Writing Wizard will start. You will be prompted for a name for the CD – this can be left at the default date. Click Next to start copying.

8 Wait for the files to be written – it is slower than copying files within the hard drive. When the wizard has finished, it will normally eject the CD. (Automatic eject after writing is an option that can be turned off.)

4

Writing to a CD (cont.)

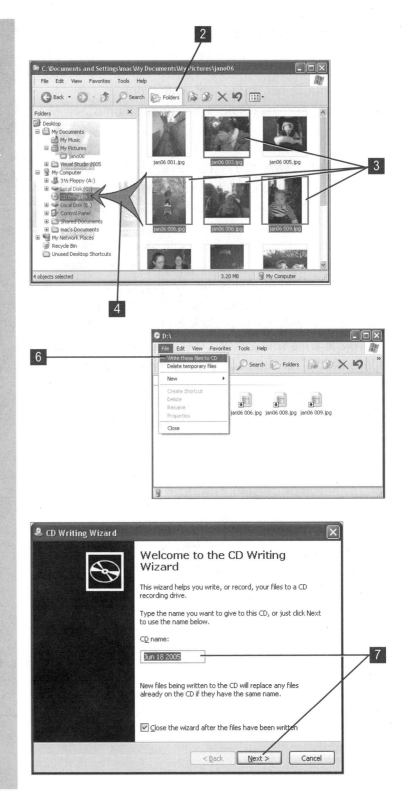

Further word processing

Introduction

You can do so much more with Word than simply type and edit text. Word has full page layout facilities – so much so that people sometimes use it to produce books. (Though in truth, it's not the software that most typesetters use if they have any choice!) But it is regularly used to produce newsletters, brochures, greetings cards, menus, advertisements and all manner of documents where appearance and style matter.

In this chapter we will explore some of Word's more advanced formatting and layout facilities. Try them out. Some you will never use again, but some you will find very handy.

And do check out the mail merge. You can save yourself a lot of time and effort next Christmas if you use mail merge to produce the labels for the cards' envelopes – or even, dare I suggest it, to personalise that 'roundup of the year' that you send out with the cards.

What you'll do

Format with the Font dialog box

Set the line spacing

Indent text

Set tabs

Work with styles

Use bullets and numbers

Add headers and footers

Correct errors automatically

Control AutoFormatting

Use Autoformats

Check your spelling

Set spelling and grammar options

Apply a border

Apply shading

Apply a page border

Create a table

Format a table

Modify a table

Insert symbols and special characters

Insert pictures

Insert clip art

Format pictures

Draw pictures

Use columns

Run a mail merge

Formatting with the Font dialog box

▶

If you want to set several font options at the same time – perhaps to make a heading larger, bold and in a different font – or you want to set one of the less-used options, you can do it through the Font dialog box. Here's how.

---

1 Select the text to be formatted.

2 Open the Format menu and select Font...

3 At the Font dialog box, make sure that you are on the Font tab.

4 Set the font, style, size and/or other options as required.

5 Check the Preview and adjust the settings if necessary.

6 Click OK.

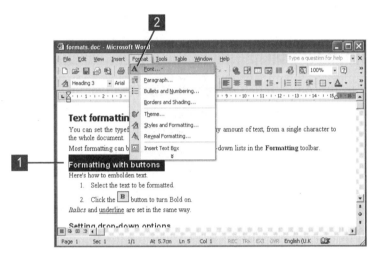

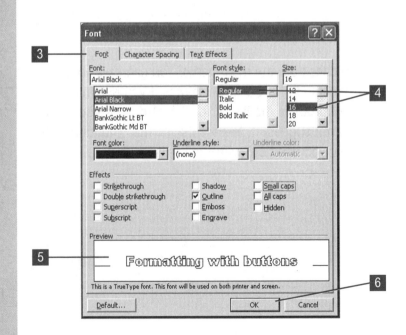

Line spacing refers to the amount of vertical space between lines of text. The default is for single spacing, which is fine for most purposes. If you need more space, either to create a particular visual effect or to leave room for people to add notes on the printout, then it can be set to 1.5 lines, double spacing or other specific settings.

The spacing can only be set through the Paragraph dialogue box.

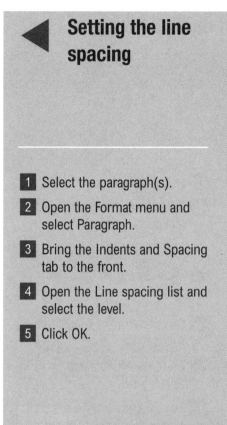

Setting the line spacing

1. Select the paragraph(s).

2. Open the Format menu and select Paragraph.

3. Bring the Indents and Spacing tab to the front.

4. Open the Line spacing list and select the level.

5. Click OK.

Important

Line spacing can only be applied to whole paragraphs. Remember that a paragraph is selected if any part of it is selected or it contains the insertion point.

Indenting text

Indents set the distance from the edge of the page margins. They can also be used to create a structure of headings and subheadings.

The left indent can be set with the buttons – each click pushes the text in (or out) 5mm. If you want to indent from the right, or set a different left indent on the first line, you need to use the Paragraph dialogue box.

1 Select the text.

2 Click [icon] to increase the indent.

   or

3 Click [icon] to pull back out.

   or

4 Open the Format menu and select Paragraph.

5 Go to the Indents and Spacing tab.

6 Type values, or use the scroll arrows to set the Left and/or Right indents.

7 To set a different indent for the first line, drop-down the Special list and select First Line or Hanging, then set the distance.

8 Click [OK].

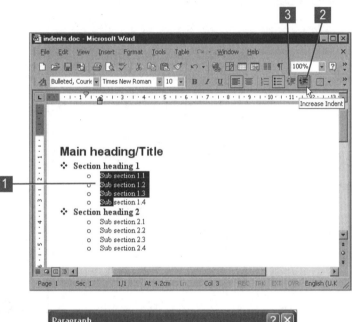

Setting indents with the ruler

Though Indents can be set more accurately by typing values into the Indents and Spacing tab of the Paragraph dialog box, it is quicker and simpler to use the indent markers on the ruler.

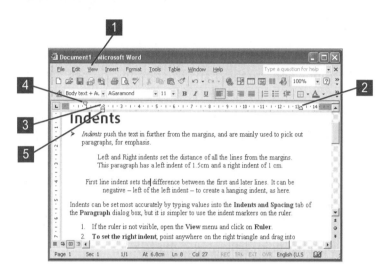

1. If the ruler is not visible, open the View menu and click on Ruler.

2. To set the right indent, point anywhere on the right triangle and drag into position.

3. To set the left indent, drag on the lower left triangle.

4. To set the first line indent, drag on the upper left triangle.

5. To move the left and first line indents together, drag on the square beneath the left indent triangle.

Setting tabs ▶

If you are writing a price list, CV or similar where text or figures needs to be in accurate columns, you should use tabs.

By default, the tabs are at ½ inch (1.2 cm) intervals and left aligned. The position and the style of the tabs can be easily changed.

When you press [Tab], the insertion point moves to the next tab position, pushing any existing text across with it.

Tab styles

Setting tabs

1 If the ruler is not present, open the View menu and tick Ruler.

2 Select the text for which you want to set tabs.

3 The current tab style is shown at the left of the ruler. To change the style, keep clicking the icon until you see the style you want.

4 Click on the ruler to place the tab. The default ½ inch interval tabs to its left will be removed.

5 To move a tab, click on it and drag it into its new place.

6 Repeat steps 3 to 5 to set any other tabs for the selected block of text.

7 Click anywhere in the working area to deselect the text.

L	Left edge of the text aligns with the tab.
⊥	Text centres on the tab.
⌐	Right edge of the text aligns with the tab.
⊥	Decimal points align with the tab.
I	Bar tab draws a vertical line at the tab point.

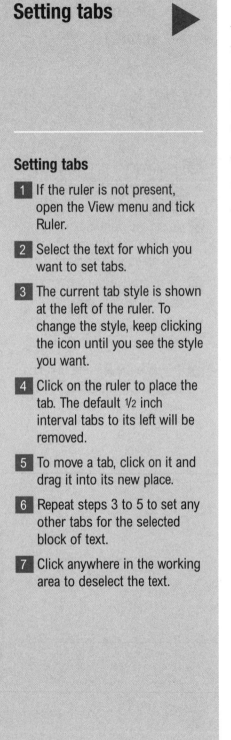

A style is a combination of font, size, alignment and indent options. Word has a range of pre-defined styles, and you can modify these or add your own. Applying a style is a matter of a couple of clicks; creating a new style is almost as simple.

◀ **Working with styles**

To apply a style

1. Select the text – normally one or more whole paragraphs.

2. Pick a style from the drop-down Styles list.

   or

3. Click More... to open the styles list in the Task Pane.

4. In the Show box, select All styles.

5. Pick from the long list.

Important !

Most styles are intended to be applied to whole paragraphs; others are 'character styles' which are for use with selected text.

5

Working with styles (cont.)

To modify a style

1. Open Styles and Formatting in the Task Pane.

2. Pick a style.

3. Click its down arrow and select Modify.

4. Edit the main format settings if required.

5. For more extensive changes, click the Format button and select an aspect to open its dialog box.

6. Click [OK].

To create a style

7. At the Style dialog box, click [New Style].

8. For the Style type, select Character if you want to use this on selected text within a paragraph, otherwise select Paragraph.

9. Type in a Name then follow steps 3 to 6.

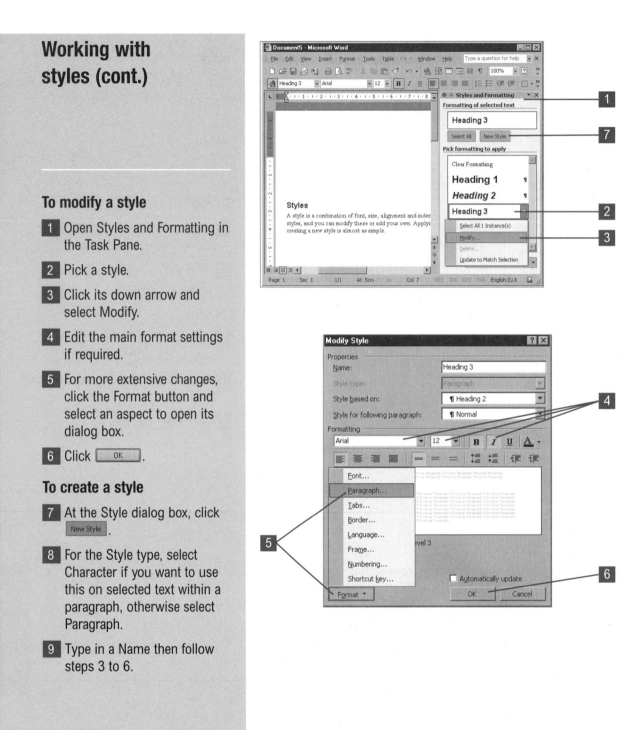

You can quickly add numbers or bullets to each item in a list by clicking 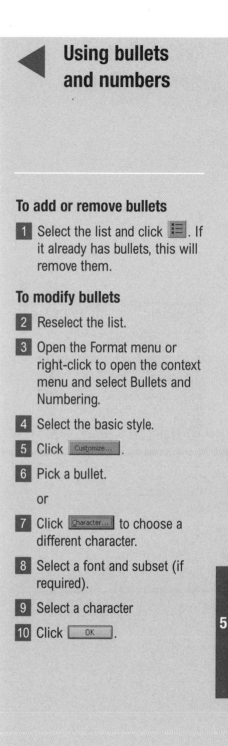 or 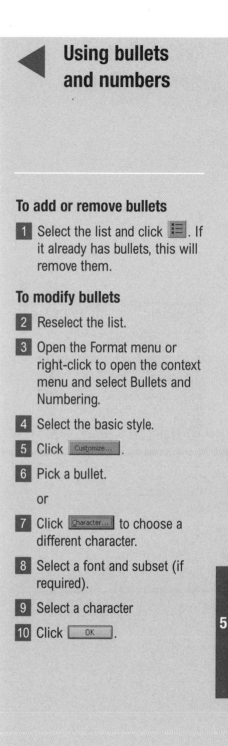. This will set the default bullet or number style, but these can easily be changed if you want to give your list a special look.

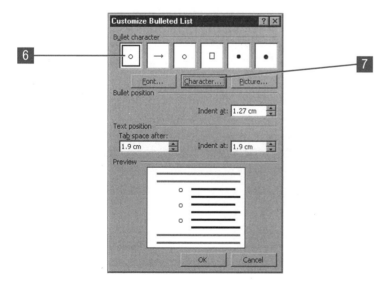

To add or remove bullets

1 Select the list and click 📋. If it already has bullets, this will remove them.

To modify bullets

2 Reselect the list.

3 Open the Format menu or right-click to open the context menu and select Bullets and Numbering.

4 Select the basic style.

5 Click Customize... .

6 Pick a bullet.

or

7 Click Character... to choose a different character.

8 Select a font and subset (if required).

9 Select a character

10 Click OK .

5

Using bullets and numbers (cont.)

Important

Word may be set to produce numbered or bulleted lists automatically – these are AutoFormatting options. See page 124.

Headers and footers appear at the top and bottom of every page. They can display the page number, date and time, filename, author and similar file details, or any typed text.

The page number, date, and other details can be produced by field codes. These are replaced by the appropriate information when inserted into the pages, and are updated as necessary. For example, the Page # field code produces the correct page number on each page.

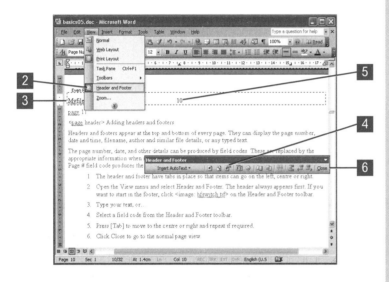

Header/footer tools

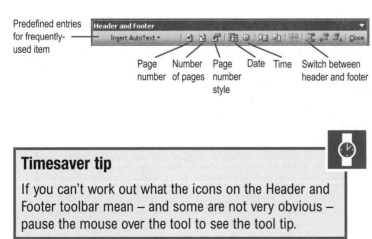

Predefined entries for frequently-used item

Page number | Number of pages | Page number style | Date | Time | Switch between header and footer

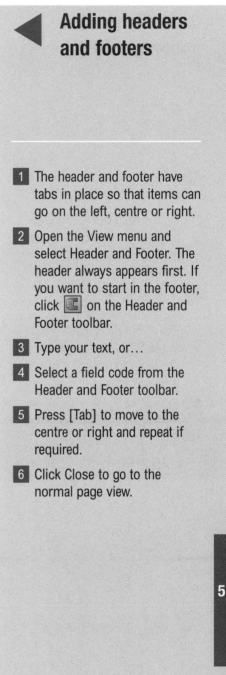

► Adding headers and footers

1 The header and footer have tabs in place so that items can go on the left, centre or right.

2 Open the View menu and select Header and Footer. The header always appears first. If you want to start in the footer, click 🔳 on the Header and Footer toolbar.

3 Type your text, or…

4 Select a field code from the Header and Footer toolbar.

5 Press [Tab] to move to the centre or right and repeat if required.

6 Click Close to go to the normal page view.

5

Timesaver tip

If you can't work out what the icons on the Header and Footer toolbar mean – and some are not very obvious – pause the mouse over the tool to see the tool tip.

Correcting errors automatically ▶

1. Open the Tools menu and select AutoCorrect.

2. On the AutoCorrect tab, tick those checkboxes where you want Word to make the correction.

3. If you turn on Replace as you type, you can add your own typos. Put the expected typo in the Replace filed, and what you want to replace it with in the With field.

4. Click 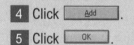 .

5. Click OK .

Word likes to be helpful. You can get it to watch your typing and correct some common errors as they occur. For instance, I routinely type 'hte' when I mean 'the', but Word knows what I mean and it will replace my mistype with the correct word as soon as I have finished it. (Which meant that I have to trick it if I actually want to write 'hte'.)

You can select which sorts of errors to correct, and add your own common typos to its list of corrections.

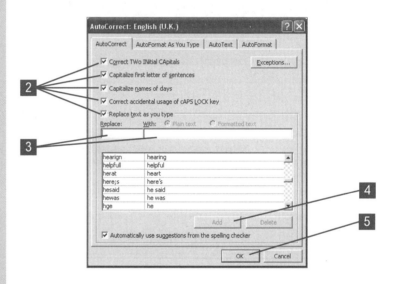

Timesaver tip

If there are any long names or phrases which you use regularly, e.g. the name of your football team, you could add them to your AutoCorrect list, using initials or shortforms in the Replace field. Then next time you are writing a letter to a chum complaining about their performance at the last match, you would type WW each time instead of Wolverhampton Wanderers (or whatever).

Word can also reformat things properly as you type. For example, it can turn fractions typed like this 1/2 into special fraction characters like this ½, or when you start to type a numbered list, it can take over the numbering for you after the first line. The options are on the AutoFormat tab of the AutoCorrect dialogue box.

1 Open the Tools menu and select AutoCorrect.

2 Switch to the AutoFormat As You Type tab.

3 Tick those checkboxes where you want Word to apply formatting as you type, or to replace characters as they are typed.

4 Click [OK].

Using Autoformats ▶

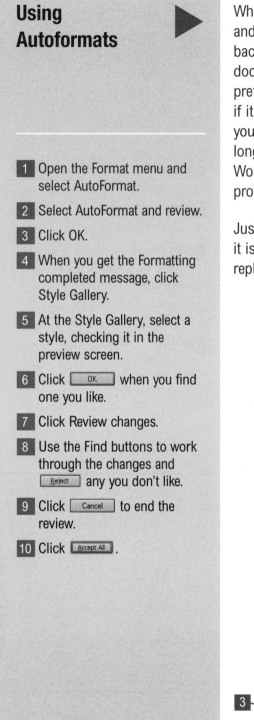

1. Open the Format menu and select AutoFormat.

2. Select AutoFormat and review.

3. Click OK.

4. When you get the Formatting completed message, click Style Gallery.

5. At the Style Gallery, select a style, checking it in the preview screen.

6. Click [OK] when you find one you like.

7. Click Review changes.

8. Use the Find buttons to work through the changes and [Reject] any you don't like.

9. Click [Cancel] to end the review.

10. Click [Accept All].

When word-processors added facilities for fancy fonts and layouts, productivity in many offices took a great leap backwards. Instead of simply typing and printing their documents, people spent time – often too much – prettying them up. Not enough people asked themselves if it was really worth the effort. The trouble is, if you want your documents to look 'professional', plain typing will no longer do. But don't worry, here's a great leap forward. Word can format your documents for you, giving a professional result, instantly.

Just to confuse you, Word calls this AutoFormatting, and it is not the same as the AutoFormatting that corrects and replaces as you type!

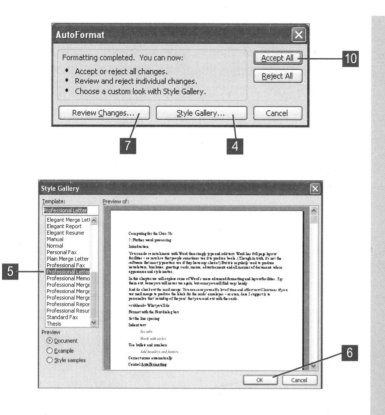

5

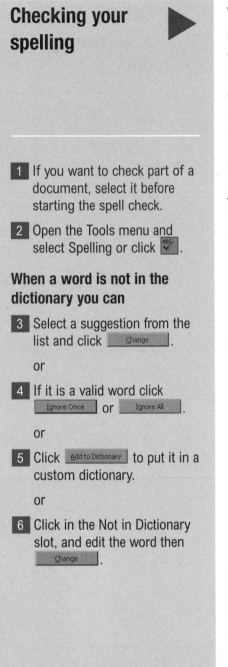

Checking your spelling

1. If you want to check part of a document, select it before starting the spell check.

2. Open the Tools menu and select Spelling or click 🔤.

When a word is not in the dictionary you can

3. Select a suggestion from the list and click Change.

   or

4. If it is a valid word click Ignore Once or Ignore All.

   or

5. Click Add to Dictionary to put it in a custom dictionary.

   or

6. Click in the Not in Dictionary slot, and edit the word then Change.

Word, like all modern applications that handle text, has a spell checker that compares your words with those in its dictionary. Word comes supplied with a good dictionary, but it does not cover everything. Proper names, technical and esoteric words may not be recognised and so will be classed as 'errors'. These can be added to your own custom dictionary, so that they are not seen as errors in future.

Word has a check-as-you-type option. You may prefer to just run a spell check after you have finished – especially if you have a lot to do and need to watch the keyboard rather than the screen!

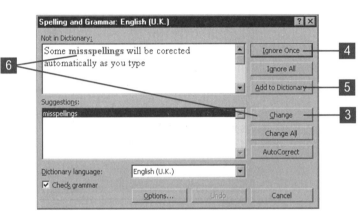

Timesaver tip

If you haven't already set up a dictionary for your own special words, click the Options button to open the Spelling options panel and use the Custom Dictionaries button.

Word can check the grammar of a document as well as its spelling, and for both spelling and grammar there are a number of options that you can set to adjust the way they work. Probably the key option is whether or not to check as you type – some people will find that it interrupts their flow.

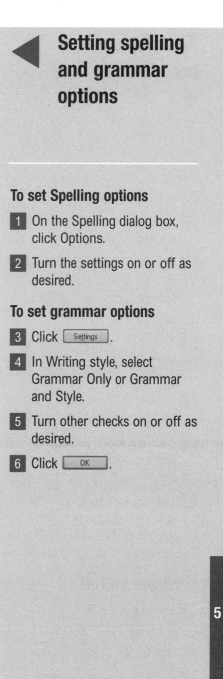

◀ **Setting spelling and grammar options**

To set Spelling options

1 On the Spelling dialog box, click Options.

2 Turn the settings on or off as desired.

To set grammar options

3 Click Settings.

4 In Writing style, select Grammar Only or Grammar and Style.

5 Turn other checks on or off as desired.

6 Click OK.

5

Did you know?

Word can tell you the 'readability' level of a document. A readability of Grade 7 (a reading age of 12) is a good level for an adult audience – any lower is patronising, but higher is hard work for most people. The *Daily Mail* has a reading age of 12; the *Sun's* reading age is around 8.

Applying a border ▶

Borders and shading can be very good ways to emphasise items in a document. They are normally applied to whole paragraphs, though there is nothing to stop you adding a border or a background shade – or both – to a word or phrase within a paragraph.

Borders can be applied and formatted using the Tables and Borders toolbar – but note that you must set the formats first. You can change the formatting after the border is in place using the Borders and Shading dialog box. This has some additional formatting options.

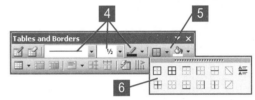

To add a border

1 Select the text or paragraph(s).

2 Click the Tables and Borders tool ⊞ on the Standard toolbar to display the Tables and Borders toolbar.

3 The Draw Table tool will be selected – click on it to switch it off.

4 Choose the Line Style, Weight and Colour required.

5 Click the arrow beside the Borders tool to display the bordering options.

6 Click an icon to select which sides the border is to be applied to. Note that the inside options only apply to tables.

To format an existing border (see below)

1 Select the bordered text.

2 Open the Format menu and select Borders and Shading…

3 Bring the Borders tab to the front.

4 Choose a Setting – Box, Shadow or 3-D.

5 Set the line Style, Colour and Width.

6 Click [OK].

To remove a border

7 Select the text or paragraph(s).

8 Display the Borders toolbar.

9 Open the border options palette and click No Border to remove the existing borders.

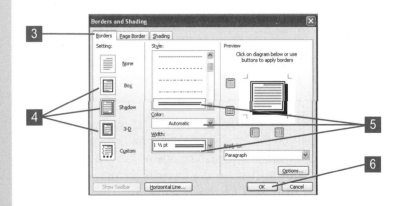

You can apply Shading to selected text or whole paragraphs, using the tool on the Tables and Borders toolbar and the tab in the Borders and Shading dialogue box.

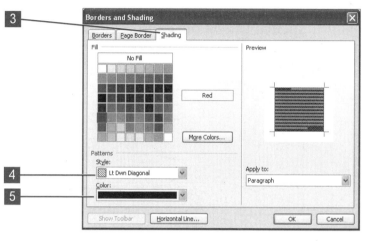

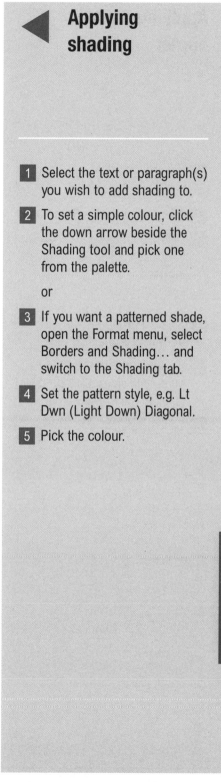

Applying shading

1 Select the text or paragraph(s) you wish to add shading to.

2 To set a simple colour, click the down arrow beside the Shading tool and pick one from the palette.

   or

3 If you want a patterned shade, open the Format menu, select Borders and Shading... and switch to the Shading tab.

4 Set the pattern style, e.g. Lt Dwn (Light Down) Diagonal.

5 Pick the colour.

Did you know?

If you need a fancy line to mark off a section in a document, you will find a selection in the Horizontal

Line options in the Borders and Shading dialogue box. Click the Horizontal Line... button and pick one to suit.

5

Applying a page border

If you are producing a poster, brochure, certificate or similar document, you might want to add a border around the whole page. This is easily done.

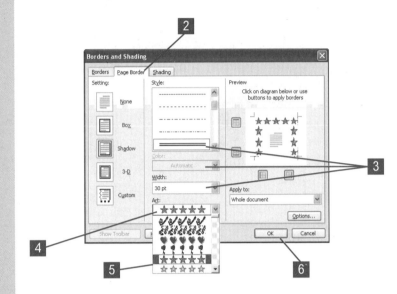

1 Open the Format menu, select Borders and Shading.

2 Switch to the Page Border tab.

3 Define the Style, Colour and Width of the line, as for other borders.

or

4 Select a decorative border from the Art drop down list.

5 If you do not want the border on certain sides, click on their icons in the Preview area.

6 Click OK .

If you need to lay out data in neat columns and rows, the simplest way to do it is with a table.

If you want to create a simple regular table, use the 🖽 button on the Standard toolbar or the Table > Insert > Table command. Whatever size you set at the start is not fixed – rows and columns can be added or deleted later.

The AutoFit behaviour sets how the table fits around its contents and within the 'window'.

■ Fixed column width – the widths stay the same unless you change them.
■ AutoFit to contents – the columns shrink or stretch so that they match the contents.
■ AutoFit to window – the table adjusts to fit the width of the page or screen (useful if you are using Word to create a web page).

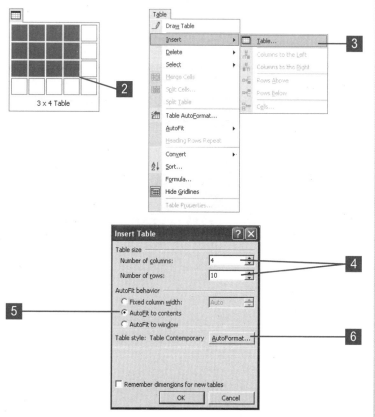

3 x 4 Table

AutoFormats are ready-made border/shading designs

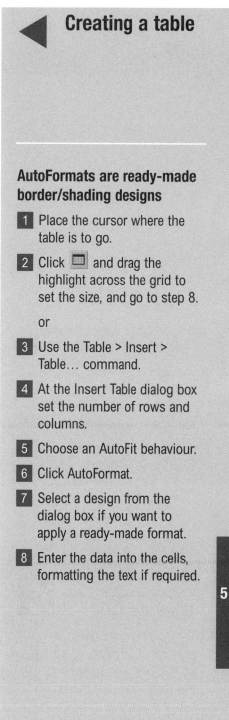

1 Place the cursor where the table is to go.

2 Click 🖽 and drag the highlight across the grid to set the size, and go to step 8.

or

3 Use the Table > Insert > Table... command.

4 At the Insert Table dialog box set the number of rows and columns.

5 Choose an AutoFit behaviour.

6 Click AutoFormat.

7 Select a design from the dialog box if you want to apply a ready-made format.

8 Enter the data into the cells, formatting the text if required.

5

Creating a table (cont.)

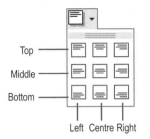

Top

Middle

Bottom

Left Centre Right

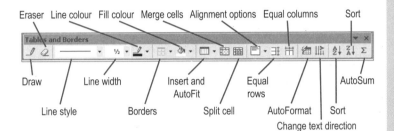

Eraser Line colour Fill colour Merge cells Alignment options Equal columns Sort

Tables and Borders

Draw Line width Insert and AutoFit Equal rows AutoSum

Line style Borders Split cell AutoFormat Sort

Change text direction

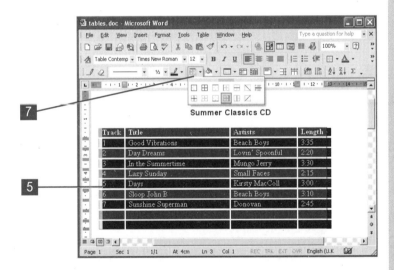

Text in cells can be formatted as normal. You can also:

1 Set the vertical and horizontal alignment of cell contents.

2 Format the borders and the lines within the table – this is slightly tricky (see below).

3 Change the background colour.

To set borders

4 Open the View menu, point to Toolbars and turn on the Tables and Borders toolbar.

5 Select the cells.

6 Set the line style, width and colour.

7 Click the Border tool and select the lines to be styled.

5

Modifying a table ▶

A table's size, shape and layout can be changed at any time – even after data has been entered into it. You can:

- Insert or delete rows or columns.
- Change the width of columns.
- Change the overall size of the table.

To insert a row or column

1 Click into a cell in the row or column adjacent to where the new one will go.

2 Select an Insert option from the Table menu.

To delete rows or columns

3 Click into a cell in the row or column, or drag across (or down) the table to select two or more rows or columns.

4 Select a Delete option from the Table menu.

To change the column width

5 Point to the dividing line on the right of a column to get the double-headed arrow then drag the line left or right to set the width.

or

6 Drag on the column marker on the ruler.

7 To change the table size.

8 Point to a corner so the cursor becomes the resize arrow, then drag the table outline to the required size.

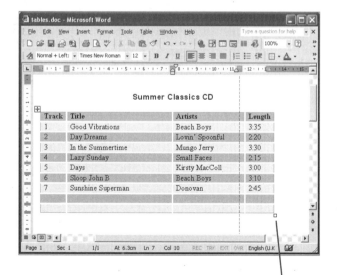

Some characters cannot be typed directly from the keyboard, but that doesn't mean that you cannot use them in your documents. You just have to get them from another source. The Insert Symbol routine lets you access the untypeable!

Inserting symbols and special characters

1 Place the insertion point where you want the character to go.

2 Open the Insert menu and select Symbol.

3 Pick a font from the list – you will find the biggest choice of symbols and graphics in the Symbol, Wingding and Webding fonts.

4 Click on a character to see an enlargement.

5 Click [Insert] to insert the selected character into your text.

6 Click [Close] to close the Symbol dialogue box.

Did you know?

There is a collection of special characters on the other tab in the Symbol dialogue box. These are mainly used in professional typesetting.

5

Inserting pictures ▶

Word can handle graphics files in many formats including BMP, JPG, GIF, Photo CD and possibly many more, depending upon which graphic converter routines have been installed. The pictures may have been captured by a scanner or digital camera, downloaded from the web, or drawn in a graphics program.

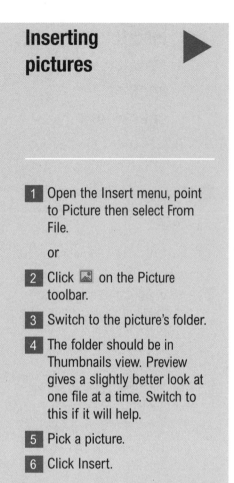

1 Open the Insert menu, point to Picture then select From File.

or

2 Click 🖼 on the Picture toolbar.

3 Switch to the picture's folder.

4 The folder should be in Thumbnails view. Preview gives a slightly better look at one file at a time. Switch to this if it will help.

5 Pick a picture.

6 Click Insert.

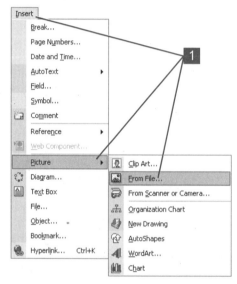

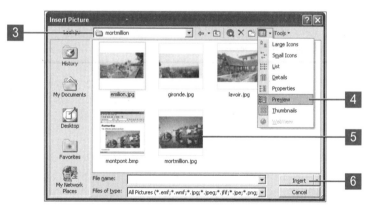

Clip art pictures can be inserted into any application – but don't overdo it. There's so much clip art around that you must use it selectively to have any impact.

Clip art is accessed through the Task Pane.

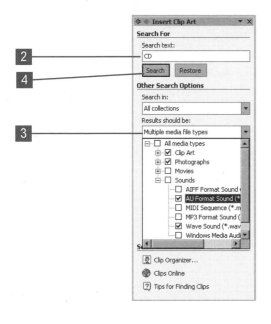

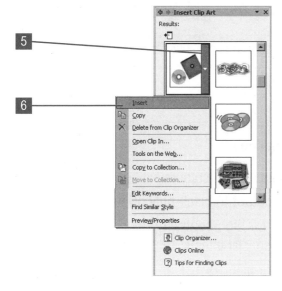

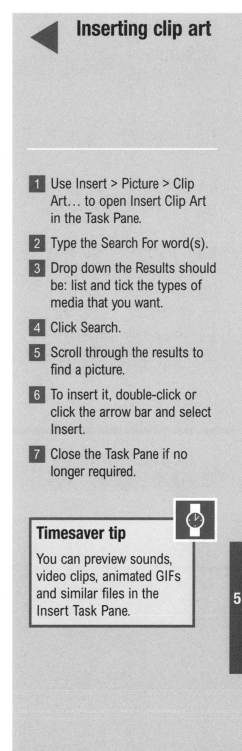

1 Use Insert > Picture > Clip Art… to open Insert Clip Art in the Task Pane.

2 Type the Search For word(s).

3 Drop down the Results should be: list and tick the types of media that you want.

4 Click Search.

5 Scroll through the results to find a picture.

6 To insert it, double-click or click the arrow bar and select Insert.

7 Close the Task Pane if no longer required.

Timesaver tip

You can preview sounds, video clips, animated GIFs and similar files in the Insert Task Pane.

5

Formatting pictures

The final appearance of any picture – file or clip art – can be adjusted at any point. Use the mouse to change the size, shape or position, or use the Picture toolbar or the right-click menu to add a border or caption, to crop it, adjust the colours, or set how text wraps around it.

1. Select the picture.

2. Drag a handle to adjust the size.

3. Drag anywhere within the area to move.

4. Use the Picture tools to adjust the settings.

5. Right-click for the context menu and use its options to add a border or caption.

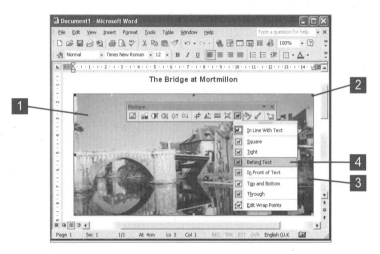

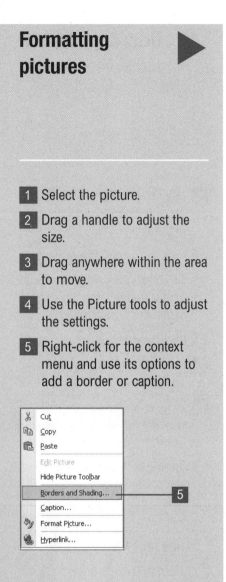

The Picture toolbar

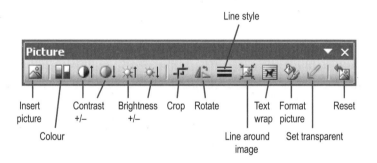

Image control options

Automatic – in its normal colours.

Grayscale – for output to black-only printers.

Black & White – for high-contrast printing, use with line-drawings or for special effects.

Watermark – ultra-pale, for use as backgrounds.

If you want to create new images, pick out points on imported pictures, or add arrows, blobs or blocks of background colour, there is a handy set of tools on the Drawing toolbar.

In a drawn picture, each item remains separate and can be moved, resized, recoloured or deleted at any later time. (Though items can be joined into Groups or placed inside picture frames, for convenient handling.) This is quite different from Paint and similar packages, where each addition becomes merged permanently into the whole picture.

The Draw menu lets you manipulate elements, singly or in groups

Selector   Autoshapes offer a quick   Line   Rectangle   way to get neat effects   Arrow   Oval

Callout – a text box with a speech/thought bubble outline

Fill colour

Line colours

Line style

Arrow style

Dash style

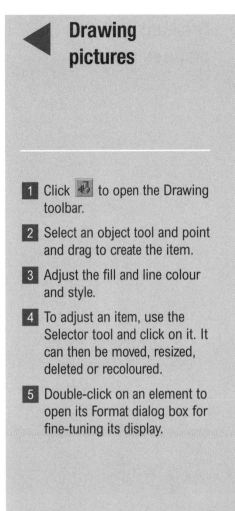

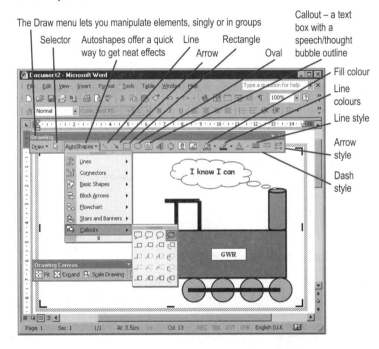

1 Click to open the Drawing toolbar.

2 Select an object tool and point and drag to create the item.

3 Adjust the fill and line colour and style.

4 To adjust an item, use the Selector tool and click on it. It can then be moved, resized, deleted or recoloured.

5 Double-click on an element to open its Format dialog box for fine-tuning its display.

5

Drawing
pictures (cont.)

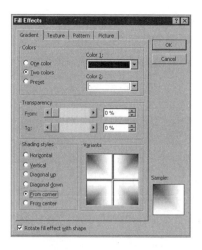

With a Gradients fill you can create a shaded background where one colour merges into another, or a single colour goes from dark to light, in a variety of patterns.

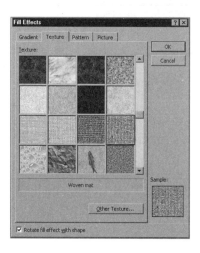

As well as patterened fills, you can also have patterned lines. Try them for distinctive frames – you can reach them from the Line Colour panel.

A Texture Fill Effects can give an interesting background to a box.

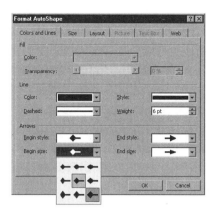

Add arrowheads from the Format dialog box – double-click on a line to open this.

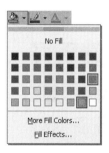

The drop-down palette has the basic colours, and access to the full palette (More Fill Colours…).

See also

The drawing tools used here belong to Microsoft Draw, a program that runs within Word (or any other Microsoft Office application). There's more about Microsoft Draw in Chapter 6.

5

Word's layout facilities are almost as good as you will find in dedicated DTP (desktop publishing) software – its handling of columns is a good example.

You can set text in two or three columns, of the same or different widths, over the whole document or a selected part.

1. Select the text to set if only part is to be in columns.
2. Open the Format menu and select Columns…
3. Select the closest Preset design to set the number of columns.
4. Clear Equal spacing and adjust the Width or Spacing if wanted.
5. Tick the Line between checkbox if a line is required.
6. Set the Apply to option.
7. Click OK.

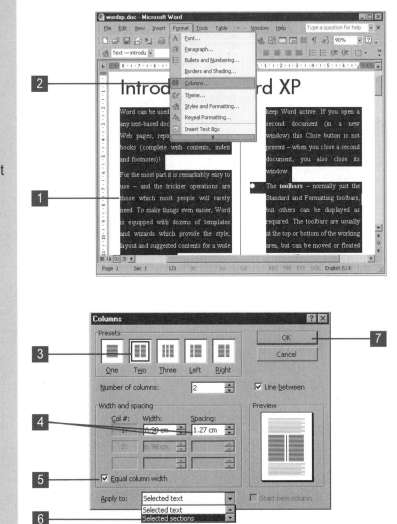

In a mail merge, a standard letter is combined with names and addresses from a data file to produce personalised letters or mailing labels. The data file can come from Access or another database system, or be created within Word. Its data is drawn into the Word document through merge fields, which link to fields in the data file.

Setting up a mail merge is straightforward, and is made even easier by the Mail Merge Wizard, which guides you through the process.

There are three stages:

■ Create the main document – typically a standard letter or circular.

■ Create the data source – which may mean typing in the data into a new file, or locating an existing file.

■ Merge the data into the document. There are three aspects to this:

1. Inserting the merge fields into the document.

2. Selecting the records to include from the data file.

3. Outputting the merged letters.

The main document

This will have all its text, apart from the name and address, and perhaps other details of its recipients. It will be formatted and have its page setup and other options set, so that it is ready to run once the data has been added.

Running a mail merge

1 When the document is ready, save it, then open the Tools menu, point to Letters and Mailings and select Mail Merge Wizard…

2 Select the document type and click Next.

3 Select the starting document – in this example, I am using the current document – then click Next.

4 If you were using an existing data file, it would be opened now. Your contacts list in Outlook or the Address Book, which holds the email addresses and other details of your contacts, could also be used.

5 If you choose Type a new list, the New Address List dialog box will open. Enter the address information for the recipients, clicking New Entry after each.

6 Click Close when you are done. You will be taken to the Save As dialog box. Give a file name and select a folder to hold the file.

7 When you get back to the Wizard, click Next: Write your letter to move to the next step.

5

Running a mail merge (cont.)

The name and address will go here

The salutation, e.g. 'Mr Smith', will go here

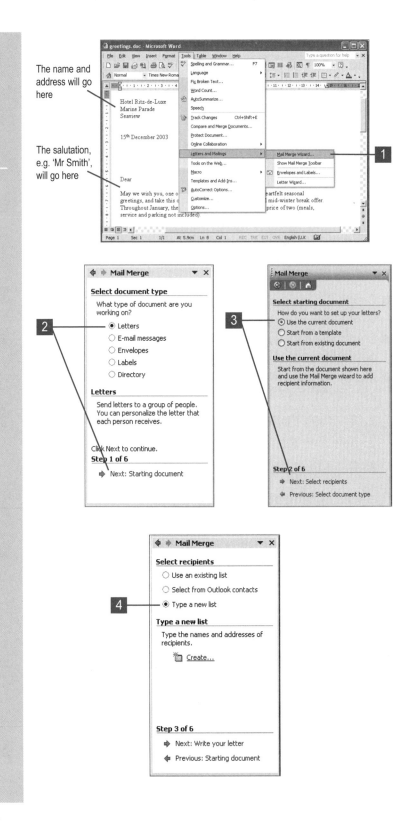

144

5

New Address List

Enter Address information

Title	Mr & Mrs
First Name	John
Last Name	Smith
Company Name	
Address Line 1	12 The Avenue
Address Line 2	
City	Hightown
State	

New Entry | Delete Entry | Find Entry ... | Filter and Sort... | Customize...

View Entries

View Entry Number | First | Previous | 1 | Next | Last

Total entries in list   1

Close — **6**

Mail Merge

Select recipients

- ● Use an existing list
- ○ Select from Outlook contacts
- ○ Type a new list

Use an existing list

Currently, your recipients are selected from:

[Office Address List] in "clients.mdb"

▦ Select a different list...

✎ Edit recipient list...

Step 3 of 6

7 ➡ Next: Write your letter

⬅ Previous: Starting document

Important

The Address List is a simple database. If you want to reuse it later, it can be edited through the Mail Merge routine before running a merge.

5

Running a mail merge (cont.)

1. Place the insertion point where you want the first field to be written.

2. Select the Address block, Greeting line or other item from the list in the Task Pane.

3. A dialog box will open. Set the options for the item as required and click OK.

4. Click Next to preview your letters.

5. At the preview stage, check through enough of your letters to see how the merge will work. If the text or fields need to be edited, do that now.

6. Click Next to complete the merge.

7. If no further editing is required, click Print.

8. Select the records to print and click OK.

9. If you want to personalise the mailing, click Edit individual letters and edit selected merged letters as required before printing.

The merge

If the letter has not yet been written, or it needs editing, the text can be typed now. This is also the time for bringing in information from the data source.

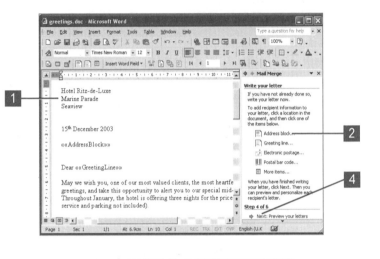

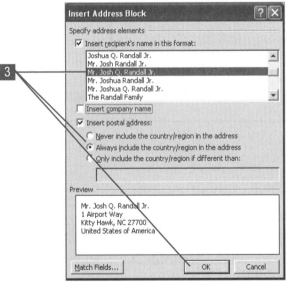

146

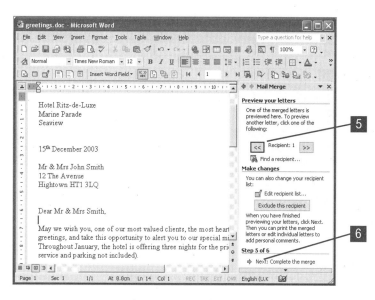

5

6

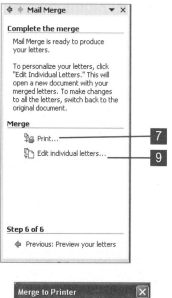

7

9

8

5

Graphics

Introduction

There are many graphics applications currently in use.
They can be divided into two main categories according to
the way images are created and stored: vector and bitmap.

With vector graphics, the image is defined by the size,
angle, colour and other properties of the lines and shapes
that make it up. These remain separate elements, and can
be selected and edited at any time. Microsoft Draw is an
example of a simple vector graphics application, and the
subject of the first half of this chapter.

In bitmap graphics software, the screen is treated like an
artist's canvas. When a line or shape or dot of colour is
applied, it becomes part of the whole picture. You may be
able to undo the last few changes, but beyond that you
cannot select a line, shape or dot and move, resize or edit it.
The picture is stored by recording the colour of each pixel
(bit) of the screen (map). The Windows accessory Paint is
an example of a simple bitmap graphics application.

As well as creating images directly on the computer using
drawing and painting software, you can also bring in
images from outside. In the last few years, storing and
displaying photos from digital camera have become major
uses for home computers. We'll look at digital cameras
and the PC in the latter half of this chapter.

What you'll do

Discover Microsoft Draw

Start a drawing

Draw the line

Use AutoShapes

Draw freehand

Rotate and flip

Add text to a drawing

Use the Picture Viewer

Use the Scanner and Camera wizard

Use image processing software

Scan with the wizard

Create a slide show screen saver

Discovering Microsoft Draw

Draw is a set of drawing tools that can be called up in any Microsoft Office application – it is not really a separate program.

It can be used in two separate ways:

■ Elements can be drawn, as separate items, in amongst the ordinary text.
■ You can create a Draw object within a document. If the object is moved or resized, then all the drawn elements inside it are moved and resized along with it.

To draw single elements, you only need to have the Drawing toolbar visible.

To display the drawing toolbar

■ Right-click on any toolbar.
■ Click Drawing so that a tick appears beside it.
■ Use this approach when you want to add a line, arrow or other simple item to your text.

For the next few pages, we will be working in Draw objects. The drawing techniques are the same whether you are working with Draw objects or single elements.

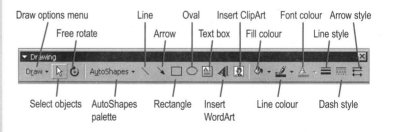

When you start a new drawing, a 'canvas' is marked out on the screen and the AutoShapes and Drawing toolbars appear. If the canvas is the wrong size or in the wrong place, it can be resized at any time and moved into place when you have finished.

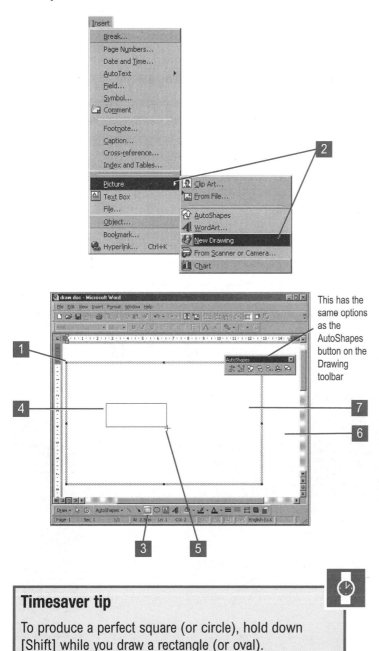

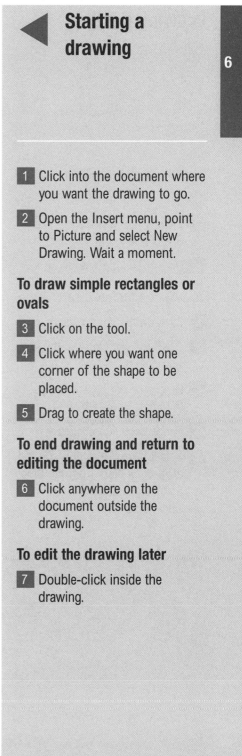

This has the same options as the AutoShapes button on the Drawing toolbar

1 Click into the document where you want the drawing to go.

2 Open the Insert menu, point to Picture and select New Drawing. Wait a moment.

To draw simple rectangles or ovals

3 Click on the tool.

4 Click where you want one corner of the shape to be placed.

5 Drag to create the shape.

To end drawing and return to editing the document

6 Click anywhere on the document outside the drawing.

To edit the drawing later

7 Double-click inside the drawing.

Timesaver tip

To produce a perfect square (or circle), hold down [Shift] while you draw a rectangle (or oval).

Drawing the line ▶

Straight lines are drawn by clicking and dragging, but remember that once drawn they can easily be resized, moved or removed.

Arrows are drawn and formatted in the same way as a line. In fact, an arrow is simply a line with a head on one or both ends, so a line can be converted to or from and arrow.

To draw a line or arrow

1 Click on the tool.

2 Click where you want one end of the line to be.

3 Drag to the required length.

To adjust a line or arrow

4 Click on the line to select it.

5 Drag on the middle of the line to move it.

6 Drag on a handle to change the angle or length.

7 To format a line or arrow.

8 Select from the options on the drop-down lists from the Line Style, Dash Style and Arrow Style tools.

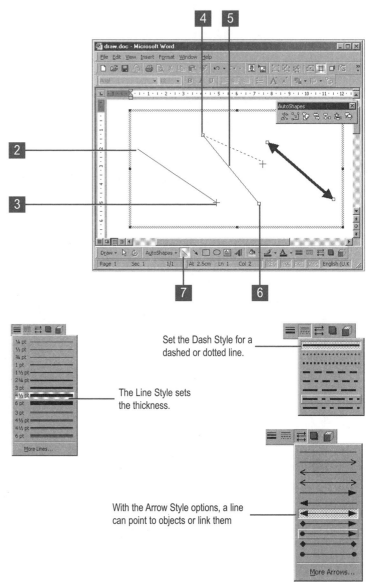

The Line Style sets the thickness.

Set the Dash Style for a dashed or dotted line.

With the Arrow Style options, a line can point to objects or link them

Simple regular shapes can be drawn from the toolbar buttons, as we saw earlier. But you are not limited to these. There are over 100 AutoShapes – patterns for a wide variety of shapes.

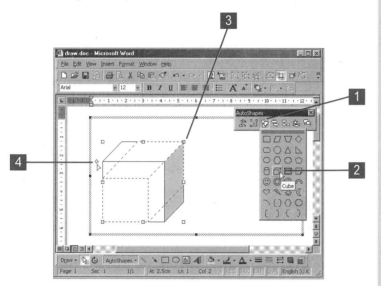

1. Click on the AutoShapes button, point to a set and select a shape.

   or

2. On the AutoShapes toolbar, click on a set button and select a shape.

3. Click and drag to draw the shape.

4. If the shape has a yellow diamond, this is a handle that you can use to change its proportions, e.g. the height relative to length. Drag on the diamond to set the proportions.

Drawing freehand

You can draw shapes by hand, though drawing smooth lines with a mouse is very hard! If there are no suitable AutoShapes, you might want to give this a try.

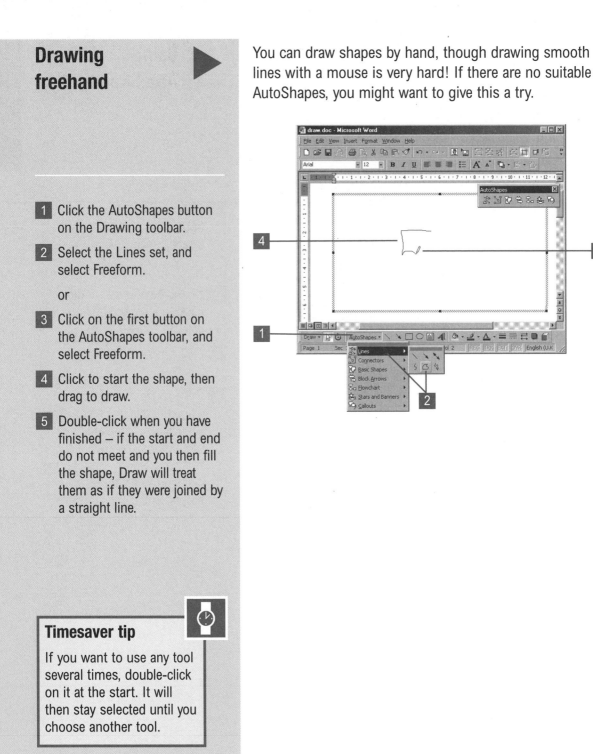

1 Click the AutoShapes button on the Drawing toolbar.

2 Select the Lines set, and select Freeform.

or

3 Click on the first button on the AutoShapes toolbar, and select Freeform.

4 Click to start the shape, then drag to draw.

5 Double-click when you have finished – if the start and end do not meet and you then fill the shape, Draw will treat them as if they were joined by a straight line.

Timesaver tip

If you want to use any tool several times, double-click on it at the start. It will then stay selected until you choose another tool.

The menu that opens from the Draw button holds options for manipulating objects, including the Rotate or Flip set.

Flip

You can flip an object in either of two ways:

■ Flip Horizontal – reflects it as if it were standing next to a mirror
■ Flip Vertical – reflects it as if it were standing on top of a mirror.

Apart from Free Rotate, these all work by first selecting the object then giving the command.

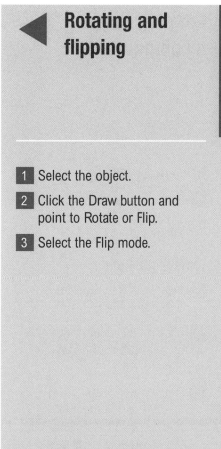

1 Select the object.
2 Click the Draw button and point to Rotate or Flip.
3 Select the Flip mode.

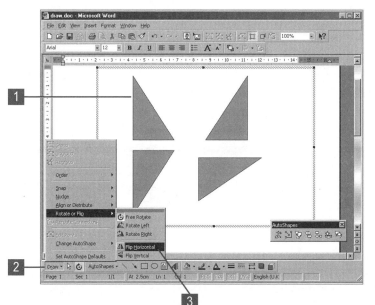

Timesaver tip

To copy a shape, select it and click Copy, then click Paste and drag the new shape into position.

Rotating and flipping (cont.)

To rotate by 90°

1. Click the Draw button, point to Rotate or Flip and select Rotate Left or Right.

To use Free Rotate

2. Select the Free Rotate option or the tool ⟳.

3. Click on the object – the green rotate handles will appear.

4. Drag on one of the green handles to pull the object round – a dotted outline will show you how it will look.

5. Click on the background to turn off the rotate handles.

Rotate

There are three ways to rotate an object

- Free Rotate – allows you to rotate the object by any amount around its centre.
- Rotate Left – rotates it 90° anticlockwise.
- Rotate Right – rotates it 90° clockwise.

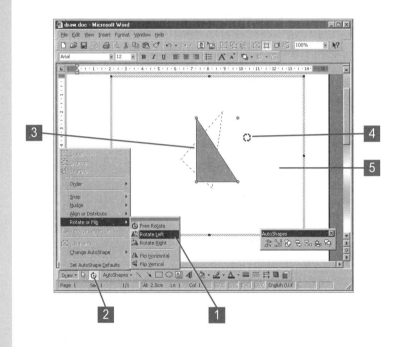

Drawn objects can be placed directly amongst text, as we saw earlier, but this is not the best way to combine text and drawings.

With a text box, you can place your text exactly where you want it in the drawing.

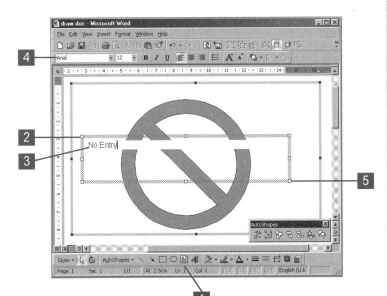

1 Select the Text Box tool 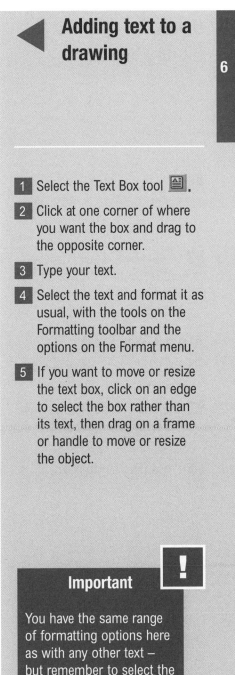.

2 Click at one corner of where you want the box and drag to the opposite corner.

3 Type your text.

4 Select the text and format it as usual, with the tools on the Formatting toolbar and the options on the Format menu.

5 If you want to move or resize the text box, click on an edge to select the box rather than its text, then drag on a frame or handle to move or resize the object.

! Important

You have the same range of formatting options here as with any other text – but remember to select the text first.

Using the Picture Viewer ▶

You won't find the Picture Viewer anywhere on the Programs menu – but it's a very handy utility. You can use it to copy, delete or print your pictures, and – of course – view them.

Once you have opened the viewer for one file, you can use it to work through all the images in the same folder.

1 In My Computer or Windows Explorer, open the folder that contains the pictures you want to view or print.

2 Double-click on an image, or right-click on it and select Open With > Picture and Fax Viewer.

To run a Slide Show

3 Click 🖳 Slide Show to start the show.

4 Click the mouse button or use the arrow keys to move through the images.

5 Press [Escape] to end.

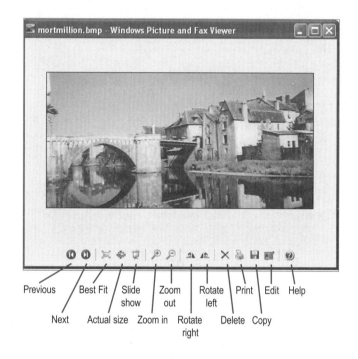

Important !

The Edit command closes the Viewer and opens the image in Paint or other graphics software.

Printing from the Viewer

The print routine takes advantage of the fact that the Viewer works with the whole folder, and not just with a single image. You can select any number of pictures (from the same folder) at a time, and print them individually or several to a page, in a range of sizes.

1 Click ⃞ Print to start the wizard.

2 Tick the pictures that you want to print and click [Next >].

3 Scroll through the Available layouts and select one, then click [Next >].

Using the Scanner and Camera wizard

Scanners and digital cameras are normally supplied with software for transferring, editing and managing the image files. The Camera and Scanner wizard is a standard Windows utility, and worth considering as an alternative. It doesn't have the sophisticated features found on most scanner/camera software, but it is an efficient and effective tool for taking images in from a scanner or a camera, and storing them in a folder.

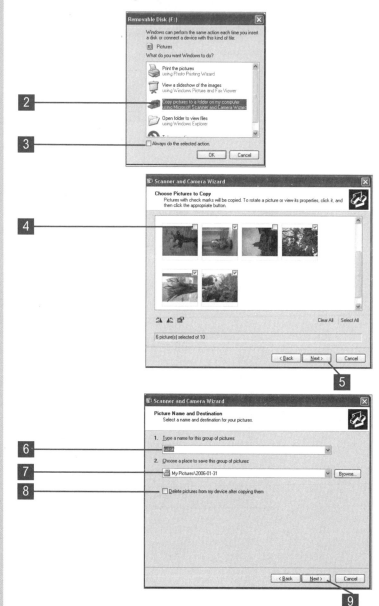

Transferring pictures from a camera

1 Connect the camera to the USB port and switch it on.

2 Windows will recognize that the camera is present, and treat the camera's memory as another 'removable drive'. It may ask you what you want to do next – select the Scanner and Camera Wizard option.

3 If you tick the Always do selected action checkbox, the wizard will start without asking next time that you plug in the camera.

4 After a short delay, you will see thumbnails of all the pictures in the camera's memory. They will all have a tick at the top right. Click the checkbox to clear the tick if you do not want to transfer an image.

5 Click Next >.

6 You will be asked for a name for the group of pictures. A number will be added to the end of this to identify each image. Leave this blank if you just want numbered images.

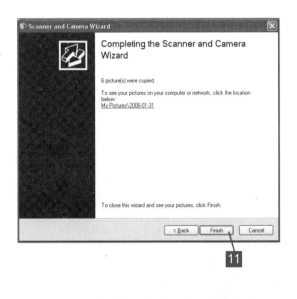

7 You will be asked where you want to store the pictures. My Pictures is the default, but the wizard can create a new folder for them. Drop down the list and you will be offered several possible folder names – select one.

8 Tick the checkbox if you want the wizard to delete the pictures from the camera after copying.

9 Click Next >.

10 The pictures will be copied across, which may take a while.

11 After the picture has been captured, you will be given the option of publishing the images on your website or ordering printed copies from an online photo printer. If you don't want to do either, move on and at the final stage of the Wizard, click Finish.

12 My Computer will open at the store folder to display the pictures. Double-click on a thumbnail to start up the Picture Viewer to see your photos.

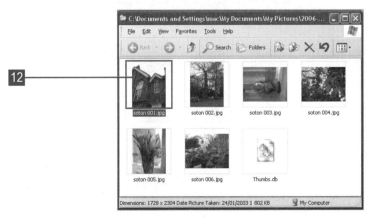

Using image processing software

When you buy a digital camera, you will get with it software for transferring images to your PC, and for editing them and managing their files. The complexity and sophistication of the software varies, but it should always include facilities for renaming, deleting and moving the files; and for rotating, resizing and adjusting the colours of the images. The examples here are from the Fuji FinePixViewer, but you will find the same facilities on you software.

To transfer photos from the camera

1   Connect the camera to the USB port and turn it on. The image processing software should fire up automatically.

2   The software generates names for the files automatically. The names start with the date and end with a number; in between you can have other text to help identify the set. As the files can easily be renamed, this is not something to worry too much about.

3   Click [Next >] to start the transfer.

4   You will see a thumbnail of each image as it is copied onto the PC. There's nothing to do here except watch and wait – unless you want to cancel and do it later.

5   The software should now have a Windows Explorer style display, with thumbnails of the images in the main pane. Select an image and explore the available commands – they may be listed down the side panel and/or in toolbar buttons.

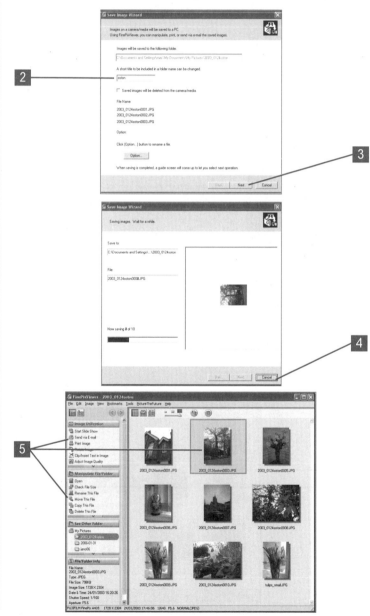

Rotating an image

If you turn the camera on its side to take a picture, the image will be on its side when you transfer it to the PC. Fortunately, you don't have to turn the monitor on its side to see it properly. Rotating an image is very simple. Here's how it works in FinPixViewer.

1 Select the picture(s) – you can rotate several at a time.

2 Click the 🔄 or use the Rotate Image command.

3 Pick a rotation – clockwise (right) or counterclockwise (left).

4 Save the new image, either replacing the original file, or as a new file in another folder.

5 Close the Rotate Images window.

Important !

This software has the option to save to another folder, rather than save with a new name because it is designed for handling images in batches. Some image processing software only handles one picture at a time, and here you would expect to find a rename option.

Using image processing software (cont.)

1 Select the picture(s) – you can resize them in batches.

2 Give the Resize Image command.

3 Select a new size from the presets.

or

4 Specify the new size in pixels.

or

5 Select Specify Ratio and enter the percentage reduction.

6 Save the new image, either replacing the original file, or as a new file in another folder.

7 Close the Resize Images window.

Resizing an image

I routinely have two versions of my better pictures – one for printing and one for emailing to family and friends. Why two? Because for printing you need the highest possible resolution, but for emailing, you want ones that will fit comfortably on a screen and where the files are no larger than they need to be. A typical 4 megapixel photo, for example, is 2,304 by 1,728 pixels on the screen and will have a file size of around 1 Mb. Most PC monitors today have a screen resolution of 1,280 by 1,024. When a 4 megapixel photo is displayed, either it will be shrunk to fit, or you will only see a quarter of it. Either way there's a lot of information wasted. If you resize the image by 50% in either direction, it will fit on screen, and the file size will drop to about a quarter – and take a quarter of the time to send by email. (And even if you have broadband and don't worry about sending times, some of your recipients may be on dial-up lines where every byte counts).

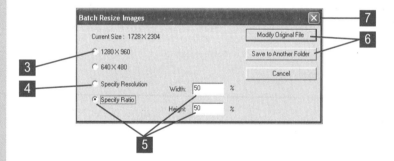

Working with colours

As this is a black and white book, I'm afraid that you're just going to have to believe me when I say that the picture below shows how tweaking the colour balances can transform an image! Most graphics software will give you four ways of adjusting the colours:

- Brightness – affects all shades and colours equally, making them all paler or darker.
- Contrast – exaggerates the differences between paler and darker shades. Increasing contrast and brightness together can bring out the details of a picture taken in poor light.
- Saturation – refers to the intensity of the colours. At the lowest setting, you see only shades of grey; at the highest, colours are very vivid.
- Hue – this is almost like moving a rainbow coloured filter over the image, turning it more yellow, then more green, then more blue in one direction, and more red then more blue in the other.

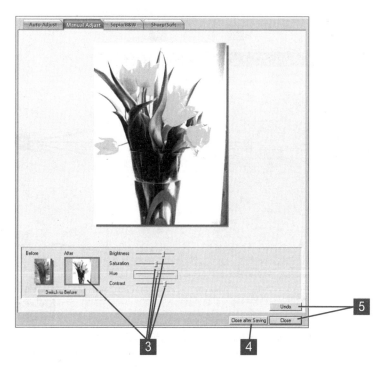

1 Select the image.

2 Look for the Adjust Image Quality (or similar name) command.

3 Drag the sliders to adjust the colour balances. The preview will give you an idea of the effect while you drag on the slider. When you release it, there will be a delay while the adjustment is applied to the whole image.

4 If you like the effect, save the changes, either as a new file or replacing the original.

5 If you don't like what you've done – and it's very easy to make a real mess of a picture – use Undo to restore the image to its original state, or close without saving.

Scanning with the wizard ▶

If you have a scanner, or a multi-function printer scanner, attached to your PC, you can capture images from that using either the software that came with it or the Scanner and Camera wizard. The wizard works in a very similar fashion whatever the source of the images, with the differences arising purely from the nature of the beasts – a scanner only handles one image at a time, and you may only want to capture part of the image on the scanner bed. The steps here concentrate on those differences.

1 Plug in and switch on the scanner. If the Wizard does not start automatically, select it from the options. It will call up the control panel for the scanner.

2 Click [Preview] and wait while the image is scanned.

3 Adjust the area to be scanned.

4 Click [Next >].

5 Specify the name, format and folder for the file in which the scanned image will be stored.

6 Click [Next >] and wait.

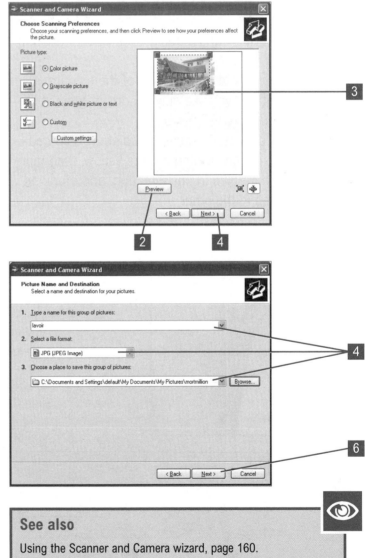

Timesaver tip

If you are scanning a full colour picture and want to send it by email or publish it on the web, the JPG format will produce the smallest file that can be viewed by email or browser software.

See also

Using the Scanner and Camera wizard, page 160.

Now that you've got all these images into your PC, it's a shame just to leave them lying there unseen. Windows has a neat little slide show facility that will give a changing display set of pictures as a screen saver.

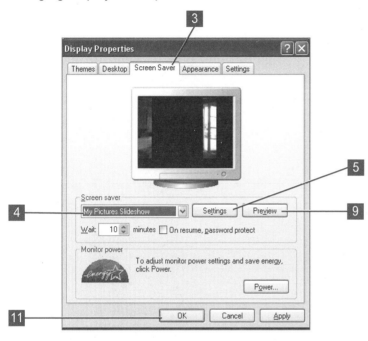

1 Locate your favourite pictures and move or copy them into one folder.

2 Right-click anywhere on the background of the desktop and select Properties.

3 Go to the Screen Saver tab.

4 Drop down the Screen saver list and select My Pictures Slideshow.

5 Click Settings.

6 At the Options dialogue box, click Browse and locate the folder where you stored your pictures.

7 Adjust the speed and size sliders, if you like. Note that you can come back and tweak these as later until you get the effect you want.

8 Click OK.

9 Click Preview to watch the slideshow. Move the mouse at any point to end the preview.

10 Go back to the options if you want to adjust the speed, size or other settings.

11 Click OK to end.

More about Windows

Introduction

In this chapter we will go a little deeper into Windows. None of this is essential for the day-to-day running of your PC, and I know of quite a few long-time PC users who have never got round to exploring any of the features covered here – and never missed it. I think they are missing out. The more you understand about the possibilities of your PC, the more you can do, and the easier you can do things. Most of the things dealt with in this chapter are ways to adapt the Windows environment so that it is easier for you to work with Read on and find out how to change the appearance of the screen – perhaps to make it more accessible, or simply to make it look the way you like it; tailor the mouse to your touch; organise the Start menu, Taskbar and the Desktop; set up the PC for multiple users; and add and remove fonts.

What you'll do

Explore the Control Panel

Set the Date and Time

Customise the display

Set a screen saver

Set the appearance

Define the screen settings

Control the mouse

Attach sounds to events

Control the volume

Set Regional options

Improve accessibility

Customise the Start menu

Create Desktop shortcuts

Tidy the Desktop

Customise the Taskbar

Move and resize the Taskbar

Use Taskbar toolbars

Create a new toolbar

Create a user account

Change user details

Use the Character Map

Install fonts

Remove unwanted fonts

Exploring the Control Panel

The Control Panel lets you customise some aspects of Windows to your own tastes.

Some settings are best left at the defaults; some should be set when new hardware or software is added to the system; some should be set once then left alone; a few can be adjusted at any time.

What is in your Control panel depends upon the hardware and software on your system. Open yours to see what is there.

1 Click the Start button.

2 Select Control Panel.

3 The Control Panel has two alternative display modes. The default is Category view, which groups the controls according to what they do. This is probably the best for new users. Click the Appearance and Themes link to see the next level.

4 At the second level of the Control Panel, you can pick a task or an icon to adjust a setting.

5 Click the Back button to return to the top level.

6 The Control Panel can also be run in Classic view. This gives direct access to the Control Panel icons. Click the Switch to Classic view link in the Common Tasks panel.

7 If you want to switch back to Category view, click the link in the Common Tasks panel (see next page).

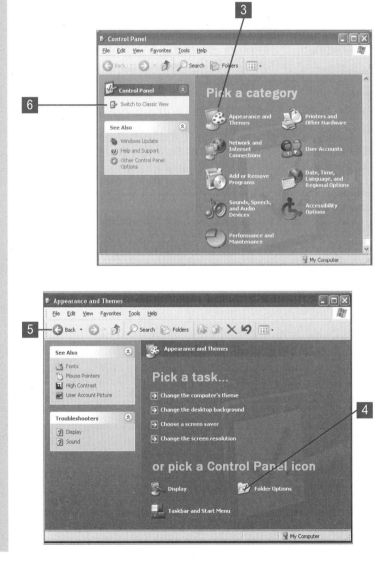

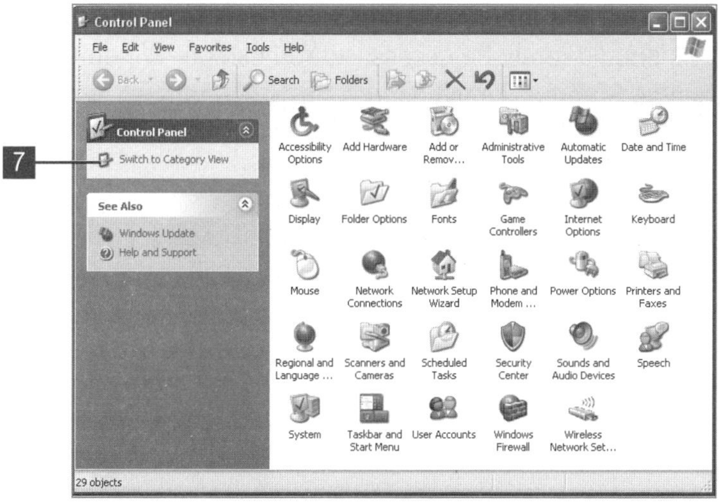

Exploring the Control Panel (cont.)

7

Setting the Date and Time ▶

The date and time can be adjusted if you want, though this should rarely be necessary. You can get Windows to handle Summer Time changes for you, and even get it to keep the clock accurate automatically.

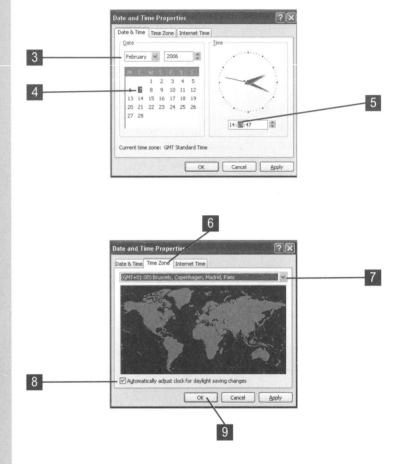

1. In the Control Panel click the Date, Time, Language and Regional Options link.

2. Select Change Date and Time.

3. On the Date & Time tab, pick the month from the drop-down list.

4. Click on the date.

5. Select the hour and minute figures in turn and type in the correct value.

6. Switch to the Time Zone tab.

7. Check, and if need be change, the zone in the drop-down list.

8. Tick the Automatically adjust for clock option if you want Windows to change the clock for you when Summer Time starts and ends.

9. Click OK to close and save your changes.

Timesaver tip

On the Internet Time tab you can turn on an option to synchronise the clock with an Internet time server. It will then check the time once a week automatically. If you are online regularly, this is well worth doing.

The theme

The display options are not just decorative. If you spend a lot of time in front of your screen, it is important that you can see it clearly and use it comfortably.

A theme sets the overall style for the Desktop – its background image, the icons for the standard Windows tools, the colours and fonts, and the sounds that are triggered by alerts and prompts. If there are parts of the theme that you don't like, you can modify them on the other tabs.

Themes have an impact on every part of the display.

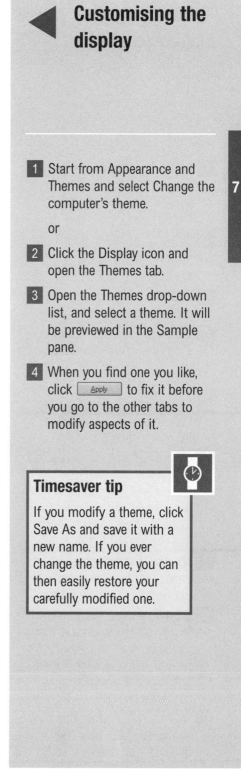

1 Start from Appearance and Themes and select Change the computer's theme.

or

2 Click the Display icon and open the Themes tab.

3 Open the Themes drop-down list, and select a theme. It will be previewed in the Sample pane.

4 When you find one you like, click [Apply] to fix it before you go to the other tabs to modify aspects of it.

Timesaver tip

If you modify a theme, click Save As and save it with a new name. If you ever change the theme, you can then easily restore your carefully modified one.

Customising the display (cont.)

1. At the Control Panel, select Appearance and Themes, then Change the desktop background.

2. Select an image or page from the list.

   or

3. Click Browse and find it on your hard disk.

4. With a large image, set the Display to *Center* or *Stretch* to fill the screen; with a small image, use the Tile setting.

5. Click the Customise Desktop button to open the Desktop Items dialogue box.

6. On the General tab you can toggle the display of the My Documents, My Computer, My Network Places and Internet Explorer icons. Turn off those that you do not use.

7. You can also select new images for the icons, and run the Desktop Cleanup Wizard.

8. On the Web tab, you can link to a web page to display that as the background – this will be updated whenever you are online and the page's content's change.

9. Click Apply to set the background but keep the dialogue box open.

The Desktop

The Wallpaper is the background to the Desktop. There is a set of designs to choose from, or you can use any image (in .BMP, .GIF or .JPG format) or a web page.

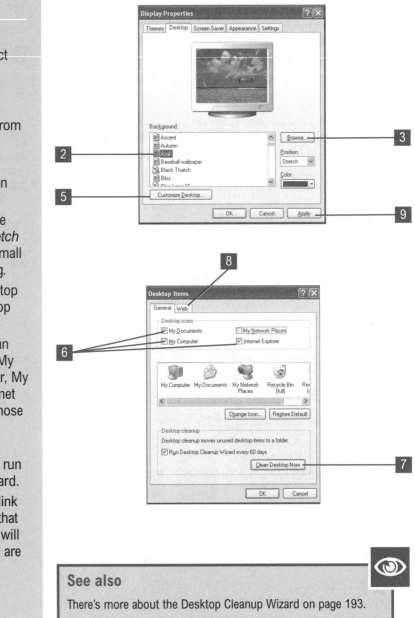

See also

There's more about the Desktop Cleanup Wizard on page 193.

Appearance

The options on the Appearance tab control the Windows and buttons styles, colour schemes and the size of fonts.

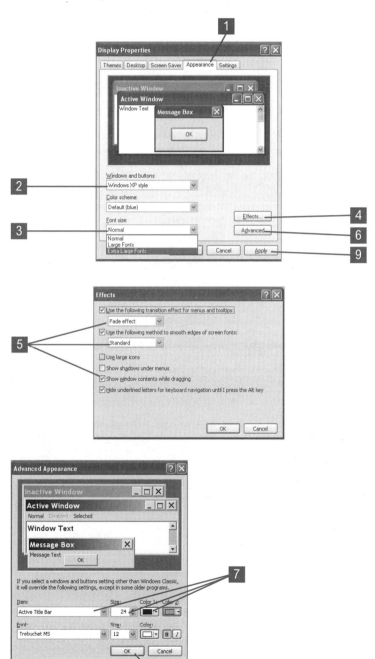

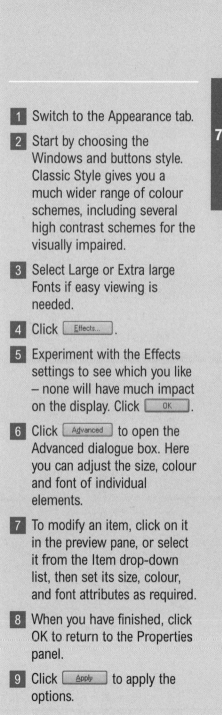

1 Switch to the Appearance tab.

2 Start by choosing the Windows and buttons style. Classic Style gives you a much wider range of colour schemes, including several high contrast schemes for the visually impaired.

3 Select Large or Extra large Fonts if easy viewing is needed.

4 Click Effects... .

5 Experiment with the Effects settings to see which you like – none will have much impact on the display. Click OK .

6 Click Advanced to open the Advanced dialogue box. Here you can adjust the size, colour and font of individual elements.

7 To modify an item, click on it in the preview pane, or select it from the Item drop-down list, then set its size, colour, and font attributes as required.

8 When you have finished, click OK to return to the Properties panel.

9 Click Apply to apply the options.

Setting a screen saver ▶

A screen saver switches to a moving image after the system has been inactive for a few minutes. These were useful on old monitors, as static images could burn into the screen if left on too long. This is not a problem with new monitors, but screen savers still have their uses. If you set it to be password protected, once the screen saver has started, it can only be turned off by entering the password – so you can leave your desk knowing that your work will be safe from passers-by once the screen saver starts up.

1. Switch to the Screen Saver tab.
2. Select a screen saver from the drop-down list and click Preview to run it on screen.
3. Click Settings and set the options to suit yourself.
4. For password protection, turn on the option On resume, password protect.
5. Click Apply to apply your choices but keep the dialogue box open.

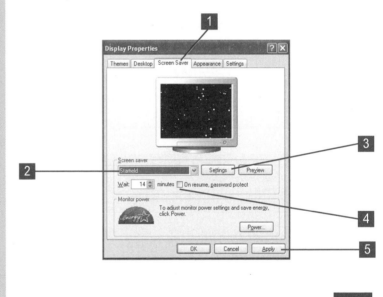

See also
Creating a slide show screen saver on page 167.

The options on the Appearance tab control the windows and buttons styles, colour schemes and font sizes. Start by choosing the Windows and buttons style: Classic offers a wide range of colour schemes, including several high contrast schemes for the visually impaired.

You should also select Large and Extra large Fonts if easy viewing is needed.

Whichever scheme you choose, you can modify it through the Effects and Advanced options.

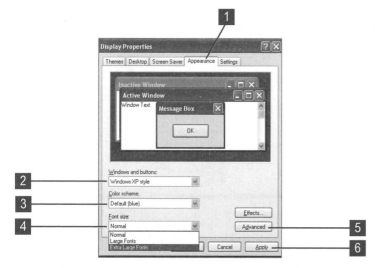

1 Go to the Appearance tab.

2 Set the Windows and buttons style.

3 Select a Colour scheme from the list.

4 Set the Font size.

5 If you want to adjust the font or colour of individual items, click Advanced and change their settings in the Advanced dialogue box.

6 Click [Apply] to apply your choices but keep the dialogue box open.

7

Defining the
screen settings

The Screen area settings control the resolution and colours of the monitor screen. Finding the right resolution for you is a matter of the balance between quality and quantity – more pixels give you larger windows but smaller type. Higher Colours settings produce a prettier screen but take more memory and time to update. Find the levels that you can work best with.

Do not change the Advanced options unless the current display is not working properly *and* you know what you are doing. You can switch to a display mode that is not properly supported by your hardware, resulting in a screen which is impossible to read – and therefore to correct!

1 Switch to the Settings tab.

2 Adjust the Screen area – try it at the highest setting first. If you do not like this, try the next one down until you reach the right level for you.

3 Set the Colour quality level. Again, start at the highest setting, and only switch to a lower one if you find that this seems to slow down the system.

4 Click Apply – the new settings will be applied.

5 A dialogue box will appear asking if you want to keep the new settings. Click No at the prompt to go back to the original ones.

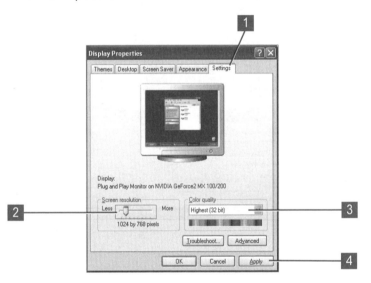

Work in Windows is much easier if you are comfortable with your mouse. Use the Mouse Properties panel to set the way that it responds.

Don't change to Left-handed unless you are the only one who uses the PC, and it is the only system that you ever use. Ideally, you should learn to use the mouse with either hand.

■ The Double-Click Speed sets the difference between a double-click and two separate clicks.
■ Pointer Speed links speed and distance, so that the faster you move the mouse, the further the pointer goes.

Find speeds that suit you and stick with them. If you keep changing them, you will never get the feel of the mouse.

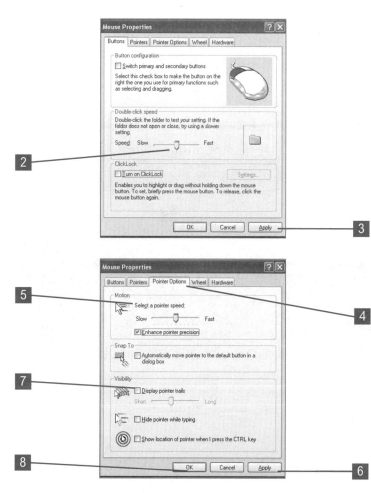

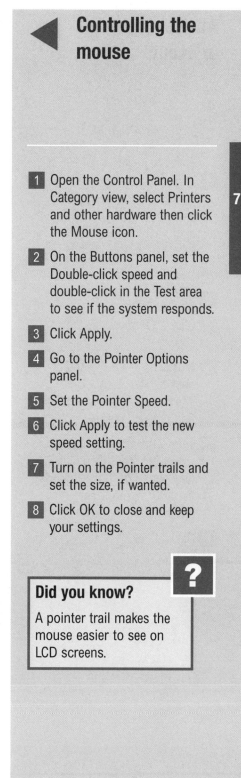

Controlling the mouse

1 Open the Control Panel. In Category view, select Printers and other hardware then click the Mouse icon.

2 On the Buttons panel, set the Double-click speed and double-click in the Test area to see if the system responds.

3 Click Apply.

4 Go to the Pointer Options panel.

5 Set the Pointer Speed.

6 Click Apply to test the new speed setting.

7 Turn on the Pointer trails and set the size, if wanted.

8 Click OK to close and keep your settings.

Did you know?

A pointer trail makes the mouse easier to see on LCD screens.

Attaching sounds to events

Windows allows you to attach sounds to events. These can be seen as useful ways of alerting you to what's happening or as more modern noise pollution. It all depends upon your point of view. I like a fanfare when the system is ready to start work (to wake me up – well, you wait so long!) but few other sounds. Try them out – the Utopia sounds are worth listening to.

The other tabs can be used to change the Audio and Voice devices or fine-tune their volume controls. The devices are best left to the system. The volume controls can be reached more simply from the 🔊 icon on the Taskbar.

1 Start from the Sounds, Speech and Audio devices category of the Control Panel and when the dialogue box opens go to the Sounds tab.

2 Pick a Scheme.

3 Select an event.

4 Click ▶ to preview its sound.

5 Sample a few more and go back to Step 2 and try alternative schemes until you find one you prefer.

6 To set individual sounds, select the event then pick a new sound from the Sounds list or Browse for an alternative.

7 Click Apply or OK .

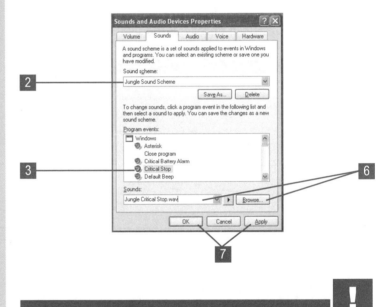

Important

You can use the Test hardware and Troubleshoot routines on the Audio, Voice and Hardware tabs if you have problems with the sound systems.

There are two levels at which you can control the volume of your PC – three if you include the knob on your speakers. At the simplest, you can use the control on the Taskbar to turn the volume up or down, or set it to mute. You can fine-tune it through the Volume tab of the Sounds and Audio Devices properties dialogue box.

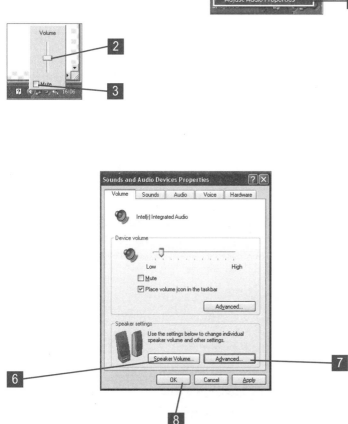

To turn the volume up or down

1 Click the 🔊 icon on the Taskbar.

2 Drag the slider up or down as required.

or

3 Click the Mute checkbox to turn the sounds off completely (or back on again).

To fine-tune the controls

4 Open the Sounds and Audio Devices properties dialogue box, as shown on the previous page and switch to the Volume tab.

or

5 Right-click the 🔊 icon and select Adjust Audio Properties.

6 In the Speaker settings area, click the Speaker Volume button to set the left/right balance of your speakers.

7 Click the Advanced button to select the speaker setup which best matches your system.

8 Click [OK].

Setting Regional options

The Regional and Language Options control the units of measurement and the styles used by applications for displaying dates, time, currency and other numbers. The choice of region sets the basic formats, but any or all of these can be customised.

1. Start from Date, Time, Language and Regional Options of the Control Panel and click Regional and Language Options.

2. Select the region.

To customise the settings

3. Click Customize... .

4. Open the tab.

5. To change any aspect, pick from its drop-down list.

6. Click OK .

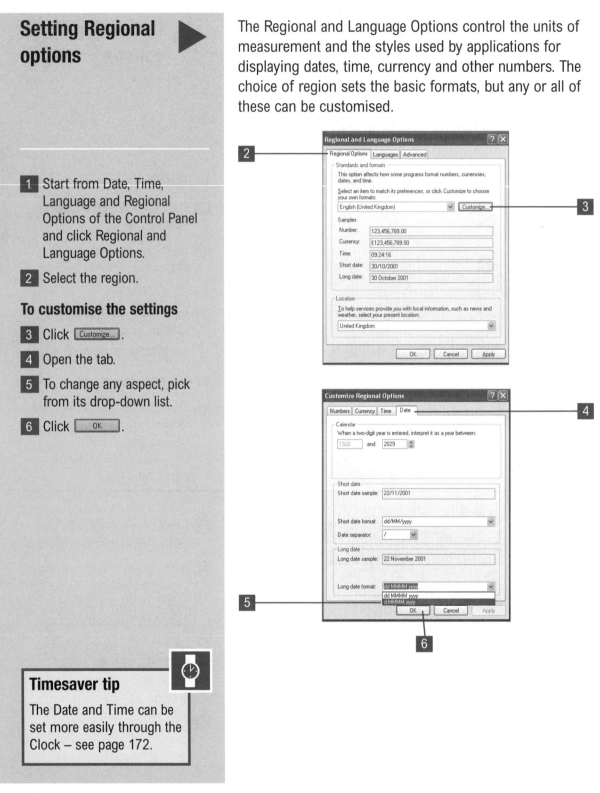

Timesaver tip

The Date and Time can be set more easily through the Clock – see page 172.

Adding other languages

Use this link if you want to be able to enter text using the keyboard for another language. This changes the letters produced by the keys and is best suited to touch-typists who are used to a foreign keyboard. Most of us are better off selecting foreign characters from the Character Map.

1 In the Regional and Language Options dialogue box, switch to the Languages tab.

2 Click `Details...`.

3 At the Text Services and Input Languages box, click Add and pick the language.

4 To define a shortcut for switching the keyboard, click `Key Settings...`.

5 Click `OK`.

Timesaver tip

You can switch between keyboards using the Language bar on the Taskbar. If you prefer, you can also define a keyboard shortcut.

Improving accessibility ▶

1. On the Control Panel, select Accessibility Options.

2. Turn on StickyKeys if you want to be able to type [Ctrl], [Shift] and [Alt] combinations by pressing one key at a time, rather than all at once.

3. Turn on FilterKeys if you find that keystrokes are sometimes repeated because you type very slowly.

4. Turn on ToggleKeys if you want to be alerted by a sounds when any of the Lock keys are pressed.

5. Click the [Settings] in any of these areas to fine tune the settings.

6. Click [OK].

Keyboard

Windows offer a range of ways to make life easier for people with sight, hearing or motor control disabilities – though the keyboard alternative to the mouse may well be useful to other people as well.

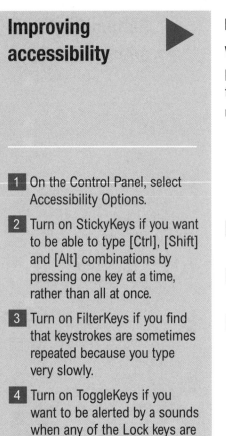

Important

You can replace the sounds that Windows uses to alert you of events with visible alerts, using the options on the Sound tab of this dialogue box.

The Display

The High Contrast displays can be selected from here, as well as from the Display panel. You can also control the appearance of that the insertion point cursor – the flashing line that shows you where you are typing text.

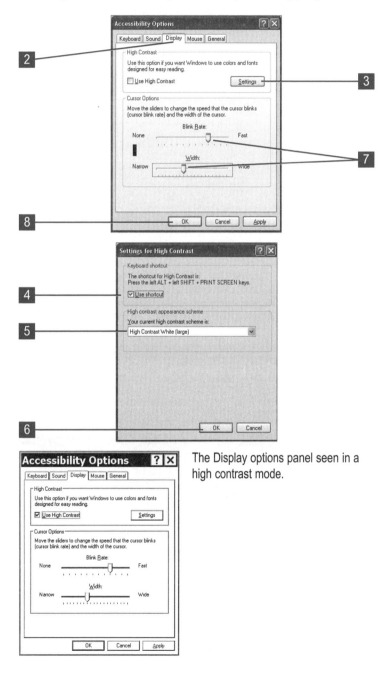

The Display options panel seen in a high contrast mode.

1 On the Control Panel, select Accessibility Options.

2 Switch to the Display tab.

To use a high contrast display

3 Tick the checkbox and click the [Settings] button.

4 Turn on the keyboard shortcut if you want to be able to toggle between High Contrast and normal displays – useful if there are times when you need a much more visible display.

5 Select a display mode from the drop-down list.

6 Click [Apply].

To adjust the cursor visibility

7 Set the Blink rate and the Width until you find a cursor that you are happy with.

8 Click [OK].

Improving accessibility (cont.)

1. On the Control Panel, select Accessibility Options.
2. Switch to the Mouse tab.
3. Tick the checkbox to turn on the MouseKeys.
4. Click the [Settings] to open the Settings for MouseKeys dialogue box.
5. Experiment to find the most workable levels.
6. Click [OK] and again when you get back to the Mouse tab.

The mouse

If the MouseKeys option is turned on, the arrow keys on the Number pad can be used to move the mouse, and the central [5] key acts as the left mouse button. It is more limited than the mouse – you can only move up, down, left or right and not diagonally – but it is easier to control.

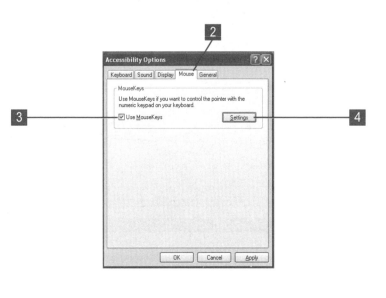

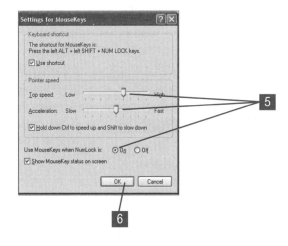

Important !

You may need to come back to this dialogue box several times before you get the mouse keys working the way you want them.

186

The General options

If you are using any of the Accessibility options, check this panel to make sure that they are turning on and off as and when you want them.

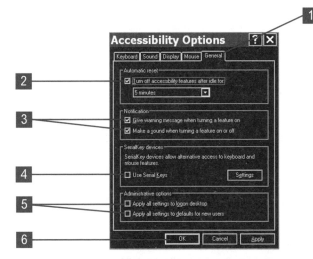

This illustration shows the standard High Contrast display setting. If required, larger fonts could be set for the panel and button text.

1 Switch to the General tab.

2 If the accessibility features are being turned on when needed by another user, then it may be useful to turn them off automatically after the PC has been idle for a while.

3 If the features are toggled on and off from the keyboard, you may want to see and/or hear an alert when this happens.

4 If an alternative input device is In use, turn on Use Serial Keys.

5 If you want to start the PC with the accessibility features active, or make them the default for new users, turn on these options.

6 Click [OK] to save the settings and exit.

Customising the Start menu

The Start menu can be customised in several ways. You can very easily change its appearance and control which items are shown in the main display. With just a little more effort, you can also reorganise shortcuts in the All Programs area, adding, moving or removing them as required.

The most dramatic change you can make is to switch to the Classic Start menu. This could be a good move if you have used and are comfortable with an earlier version of Windows. The Classic Start menu is neater, but lacks the quick links to your main applications. It can be customised in the same way as in earlier versions of Windows, with routines for adding and removing menu items.

1. Right-click on the Start button and select Properties.

2. Select the menu style.

3. Click OK.

Important

If you are one of several users on a PC, remember that every user has their own Start menu, so feel free to customise yours to suit yourself.

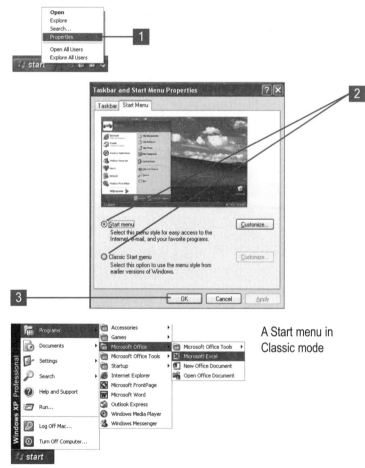

A Start menu in Classic mode

The Customise options govern the content and layout of the initial Start menu display.

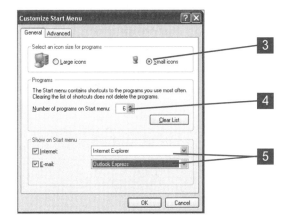

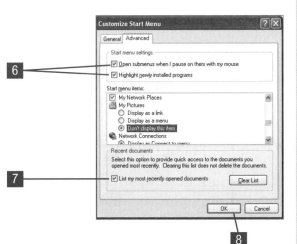

1 Open the Start menu Properties dialogue box.

2 On the Start menu tab, click Customise.

3 At the Customise Start Menu dialogue box, select the icon size.

4 In the Programs area set how many shortcuts to have in the quick access set on the left – you may want more or less.

5 Select the programs to run from the Internet and the E-mail shortcuts, or turn them off if not wanted.

6 On the Advanced tab work through the Start menu items list, deciding which of the standard shortcuts to display on the right side of the menu.

7 If you don't use the recent document list, remove the shortcut.

8 Click OK.

Customising the Start menu (cont.)

1. Open the Start menu, right-click on All Programs and select Open from the short menu.

2. When the Start menu folder opens, click Folders to display the Folder list – it will make it easier to see what you are doing.

3. Reorganise the menu system, using the normal file management techniques for moving, deleting and renaming files (shortcuts) and folders (sub-menus).

4. Click [Close] when you have finished.

Timesaver tip

If you want a new sub-menu, use File > New > Folder to create a new folder.

Organising the menu

Over time, as you install more applications, you may find that your All Programs menu becomes overcrowded. To make it more manageable, you can create group folders and move the shortcuts and folders of related applications into these. A short main menu that leads to two levels of sub-menus is easier to work with than one huge menu!

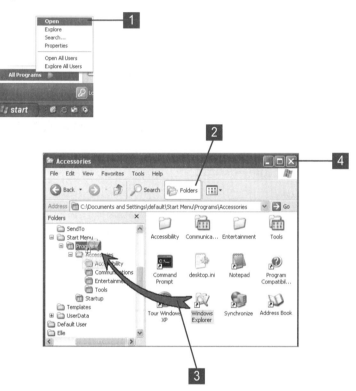

A shortcut on the Desktop can be a convenient way of running a program that you use regularly. When new programs are installed, you are sometimes given the option of adding a Desktop shortcut. If not, or you decide later that you want one, you can set up a shortcut in a minute – and if you don't make much use of it, you can remove it even faster!

Sometimes when installing **shareware** or **freeware** programs downloaded from the web, Start menu or Desktop shortcuts are not created automatically, and you will have to do it yourself. It's not difficult.

1 Open the Start menu and find the program's entry.

2 Right-click on the entry and select Create Shortcut.

or

3 In My Computer, find the program file – it will have an EXE extension.

4 Right-click on the file and select Send To then Desktop from its context menu.

5 Edit the name – it will be 'Shortcut to...'.

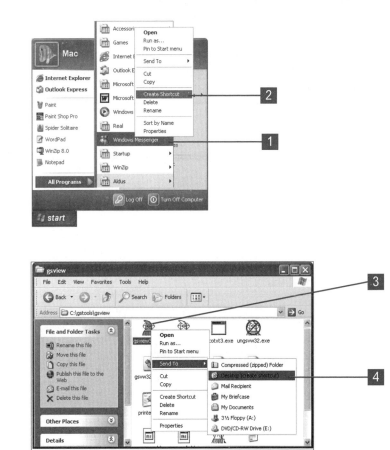

Timesaver tip

You can also create desktop shortcuts to files or folders, so that you can open them with a single click. Just right-click on them in My Computer and select Send To > Desktop.

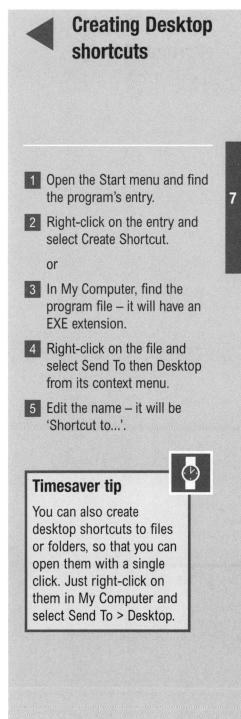

Creating Desktop shortcuts (cont.)

Too many shortcuts will clutter up your Desktop. Here are two simple ways to cut through the clutter.

■ If you don't expect to ever use a shortcut again, select it and press [Delete]. Note that this only removes the shortcut, not the program, file or folder.
■ Run the Desktop Cleanup Wizard. It will collect unused shortcuts and pack them into a folder. If you decide you need them, you can easily drag them out of the folder.

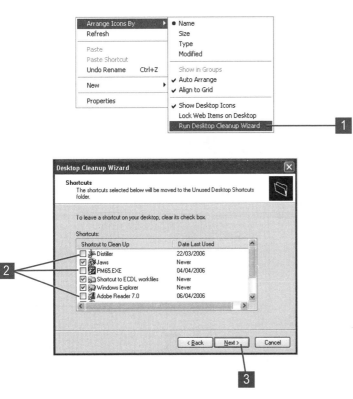

7

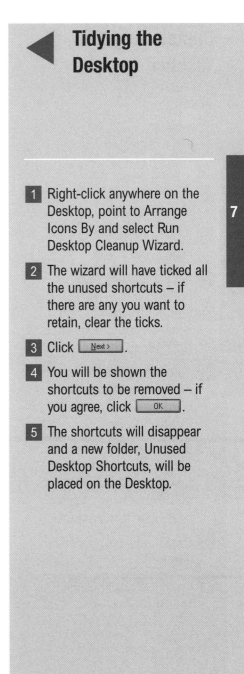

1 Right-click anywhere on the Desktop, point to Arrange Icons By and select Run Desktop Cleanup Wizard.

2 The wizard will have ticked all the unused shortcuts – if there are any you want to retain, clear the ticks.

3 Click [Next >].

4 You will be shown the shortcuts to be removed – if you agree, click [OK].

5 The shortcuts will disappear and a new folder, Unused Desktop Shortcuts, will be placed on the Desktop.

Customising the Taskbar

Many parts of the Windows XP system can be tailored to your own tastes. Some of the most important are covered in the next two chapters. We'll start with the Taskbar and the Start menu. You can adjust the size of the menu icons, turn the clock on or off, hide the Taskbar, or place it on any edge of the screen.

1. Right-click on any blank area of the Taskbar.

2. Select Properties from the context menu.

3. Set the options. Keep the taskbar on top – when off, to see the Taskbar you must minimize applications or press [Ctrl]-[Esc].

4. Auto-hide slides the Taskbar off-screen when not in use. Point off-screen to restore the Taskbar to view.

5. Group similar taskbar buttons – if the same program is running in several windows, they can all be stacked onto one button to save space.

6. Click [Apply] to see how they look.

7. Click [OK] to fix the settings and close.

Moving the Taskbar is quite easy to do by mistake, so it is just as well to know how to do it intentionally – if only to correct a mistake!

Resizing the Taskbar – making it deeper or wider – is sometimes useful. Narrow vertical displays are almost unreadable. When you are running a lot of programs with a horizontal Taskbar, the titles on the buttons can be very small. If you deepen the display, you get two rows of decent-sized buttons.

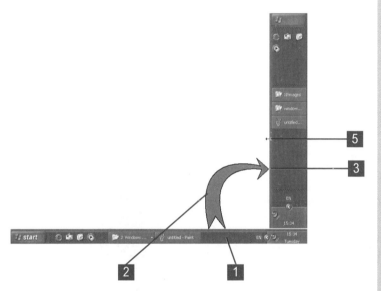

To move the taskbar

1. Point to any free space on the Taskbar.
2. Drag towards the top, left or right of the screen, as desired.
3. Release the mouse button.

To resize the taskbar

4. Point to the inside edge of the Taskbar.
5. When the cursor changes to ↔, drag to change the width of the Taskbar.

Timesaver tip

If you like to keep the Taskbar visible, it takes least space at the top or bottom of the screen.

If you have a lot of applications running at once, or several toolbars on the Taskbar, then the Taskbar is best at the left or right edge, but with Auto-Hide turned on.

Using Taskbar toolbars ▶

Taskbar toolbars are sets of buttons which live on the Taskbar. Normally the Taskbar will have only the Quick Launch and the Language bars, apart from the buttons for any open applications and the clock.

If you find that you do not use them, these toolbars can be removed, to allow more space for application buttons.

If you like working from the Taskbar, other toolbars can be added, turning the Taskbar into the main starting point for all your commonly-used activities.

To add a toolbar

1 Right-click on an empty place on the Taskbar to open its context menu.

2 Point to Toolbars.

3 Click on a toolbar to add it to (or remove it from) the Taskbar.

To set toolbar options

4 Right-click on a toolbar to open its context menu.

5 Point to View and set the button size.

6 Turn on the toolbar Title if required.

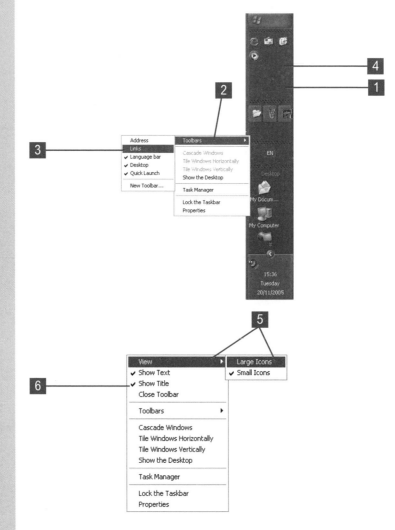

If you like the Taskbar as a means of starting programs, you can set up new Taskbar toolbars to hold your own collections of shortcuts to programs that you use regularly.

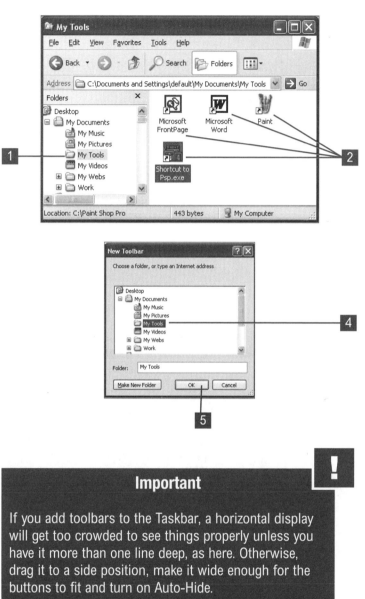

1 In Windows Explorer or My Computer, create a new folder – it can be in any convenient place on your hard drive.

2 Set up shortcuts to your main programs.

3 Open the Taskbar menu, point to **Toolbars** and select **New Toolbar**.

4 Select your new folder.

5 Click [OK].

❗ Important

If you add toolbars to the Taskbar, a horizontal display will get too crowded to see things properly unless you have it more than one line deep, as here. Otherwise, drag it to a side position, make it wide enough for the buttons to fit and turn on Auto-Hide.

Creating a user account ▶

1. Click on the User Accounts link in the Control Panel.
2. Click Create a new account.
3. Enter the user's name and click Next.
4. Set the account type.
5. Click Create Account.

Windows XP makes it easy for several people to share the use of one PC. Each user can have their own set of folders and their own customised Desktop and Start menu.

There are two types of account:

■ Limited users have access to only their own files and those in the *Shared Documents folder*. They can customise their own desktops, and decide their own passwords and the pictures which identify their account.
■ Administrators have full access to all aspects of the PC – including other users' areas.

You must have Administrator access to create accounts.

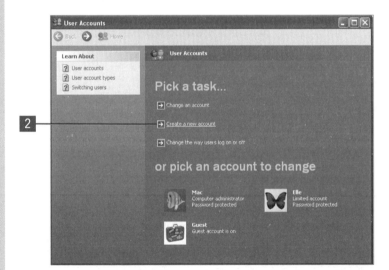

3

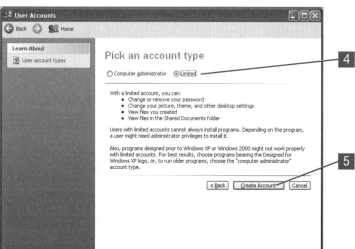

4

5

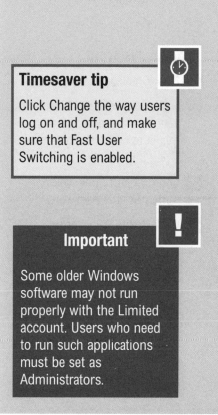

Timesaver tip

Click Change the way users log on and off, and make sure that Fast User Switching is enabled.

Important

Some older Windows software may not run properly with the Limited account. Users who need to run such applications must be set as Administrators.

Changing user details ▶

Limited users can change only two aspects of their accounts: the password and the picture which appears on the welcome screen and the Start menu. Administrator users can change all aspects of their own – or any other user's – account, including the account type. Changes can be made at any time.

1 Click the User Accounts link in the Control Panel. Administrators now need to pick the account.

To change the picture

2 Click Change my picture.

3 Select an image from the offered set or click Browse for more pictures to use one of your own files.

4 Click Change Picture.

To add a password

5 Click Create a password.

6 Enter the password twice – as you won't be able to read it, this is to check that you have typed it correctly.

7 Enter a hint to help you remember the password.

8 Click Create Password.

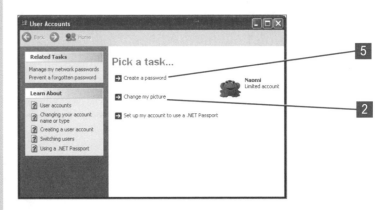

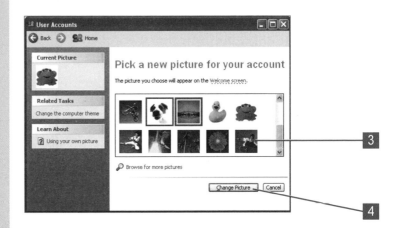

Jargon buster

.NET Passports are accepted at many internet sites that use secure systems to protect confidential data – set one up from here if you find that you need one

Important

Passwords can be a pain and should only be created if needed. If you do create one, click the Prevent a forgotten password link in the Related Tasks and create a 'password reset' disk. This will enable you to recover all your data should you later forget the password.

The password can be anything, but should be something that you can remember but that others are unlikely to guess. And the password hint should not be too obvious – it can be seen by other users.

Using the Character Map

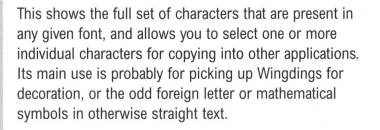

This shows the full set of characters that are present in any given font, and allows you to select one or more individual characters for copying into other applications. Its main use is probably for picking up Wingdings for decoration, or the odd foreign letter or mathematical symbols in otherwise straight text.

The characters are rather small, but you can get a better look at a character, by holding the mouse button down while you point at it. This produces an enlarged image.

1 Go to the Accessories menu and select Character Map.

2 Select the Font.

3 Click on a character to highlight it.

4 Click [Select] to place it into Characters to Copy.

5 Go back over Steps 3 and 4 as necessary.

6 Click [Copy] to copy to the Clipboard.

7 Return to your application and Paste the characters into it.

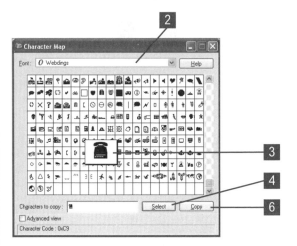

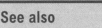

See also

In Word, you can insert special characters directly through Words Insert Symbol routine.

There is one school of thought that says you can never have enough fonts. There is a decent core supplied with Windows itself, and you will normally acquire more with any word-processor and/or desktop publishing packages that you install. If these are not enough for you, there are whole disks full of fonts available commercially and through the shareware distributors.

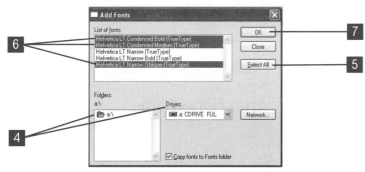

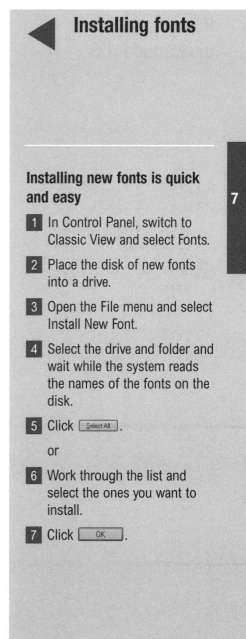
Installing new fonts is quick and easy

1 In Control Panel, switch to Classic View and select Fonts.

2 Place the disk of new fonts into a drive.

3 Open the File menu and select Install New Font.

4 Select the drive and folder and wait while the system reads the names of the fonts on the disk.

5 Click [Select All].

or

6 Work through the list and select the ones you want to install.

7 Click [OK].

Removing unwanted fonts ▶

1. Click ⒜ℬ the Similarity tool.
2. Pick a font to list by, then select and Open it from its context menu.
3. Select and Open any Very similar font.
4. Click [Done] to close the viewer.

If you have fonts that you never have used and never will, remove them. This will save space on the hard disk, but more importantly it will speed up Windows' Start Up and produce a shorter set to hunt through when you are setting a font in an application.

Listing fonts by similarity helps to identify unnecessary ones.

If it is not useful, press [Delete] to remove it.

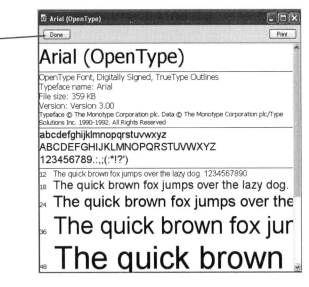

Removing unwanted fonts (cont.)

Important

There can be subtle differences between the screen and printed appearance of a font – print a sample for a closer look.

7

Looking after your PC

Introduction

A modern PC requires very little maintenance – and certainly very little physical maintenance. Wiping the screen with an anti-static cloth from time to time is about all that is normally necessary – if any component fails, there's little you could have done to prevent it, and nothing you can do to mend it (though replacement of most parts is very simple).

It's the hard disk, or rather, the data that is stored on the hard disk, which needs the maintenance. The more a disk is used, and the more data that is stored on it, the more necessary maintenance becomes. Look after your storage, and you should be able to enjoy many years of happy computing; neglect it, and one day you will find that some of your files have gone missing or become unreadable, and they may be essential and irreplaceable.

In this chapter you will learn how to keep your hard disk working efficiently, and how to back up files so that if the worst does happen and your hard disk fails, at least your data will be safe.

What you'll do

Find the System Tools

Check a disk for errors

Defragment a disk

Backup

Restore files from backups

Clean up the hard disk

Remove programs

Change Windows components

Restore your system

Keep Windows up-to-date

Add a printer

Cancel a print job

Finding the System Tools

These programs will help to keep your disks in good condition, and your data safe.

- Backup – enables you to keep safe copies of your important files, and to recover lost data.
- Disk Cleanup – finds and removes unused files.
- Disk Defragmenter – optimises the organisation of storage to maximize the disk's speed and efficiency.
- Error-check – finds and fixes errors in data stored on disks.
- Scheduled Tasks – lets you perform maintenance at set times.
- System Information – gives (technical) information about what's going on inside your computer.
- System Restore – backs up essential files, so that the system can be restored to normal after a crash.

Most of the tools can be started from the System Tools part of the Start menu; some are reached through the hard disk's Properties panel.

1 Click start.

2 Point to All Programs

3 Point to Accessories.

4 Point to System Tools.

5 Click to select a tool.

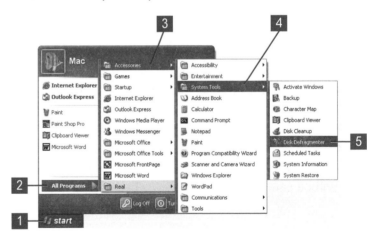

The four system tools that are needed for the routine housekeeping can also be reached from the Properties box of any disk. The messages will remind you of chores you have been neglecting!

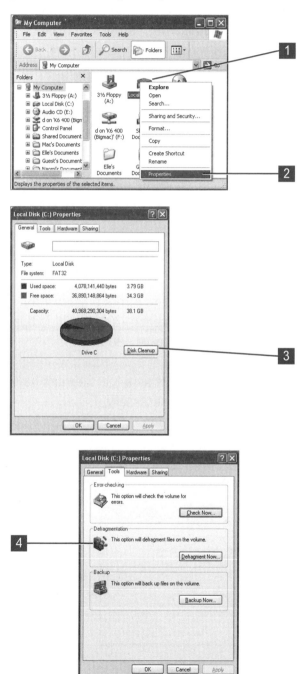

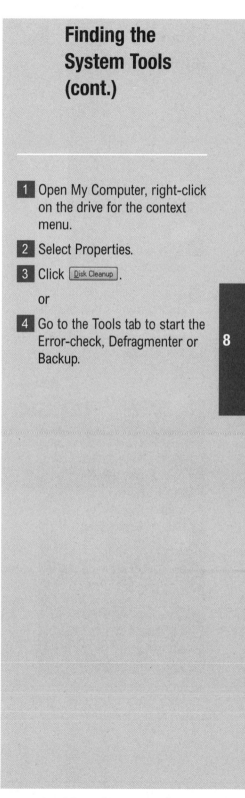

Finding the System Tools (cont.)

1 Open My Computer, right-click on the drive for the context menu.

2 Select Properties.

3 Click [Disk Cleanup].

or

4 Go to the Tools tab to start the Error-check, Defragmenter or Backup.

8

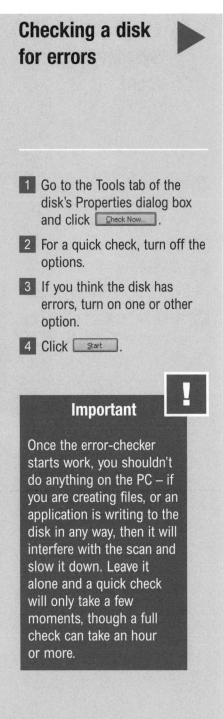

Checking a disk for errors

1 Go to the Tools tab of the disk's Properties dialog box and click [Check Now...].

2 For a quick check, turn off the options.

3 If you think the disk has errors, turn on one or other option.

4 Click [Start].

Data is stored on disks in *allocation units*. A small file may fit on a single unit, but others are spread over many. A file's units may be in a continuous run or scattered over the disk (see *Disk Defragmenter*), but they are all kept together by links from one to the next. Sometimes the links get corrupted leaving *lost fragments*, with no known links to any file, or *cross-linked files*, where two are chained to the same unit of data.

The magnetic surface of the disk may also (rarely) become corrupted, creating *bad sectors* where data cannot be stored.

The Error-checking routine can identify these and, with a bit of luck, retrieve any data written there and transfer it to a safe part of the disk. It is very simple to run, with only two options at the start, and nothing for you to do once it's running.

■ With Automatically fix file system errors on, it will try to solve any problems that it meets – and it will do this better than you or I could, so leave it to it!

■ Scan for and attempt recovery of bad sectors will test the surface of the disk, to make sure that files can be stored safely, and rebuild it if necessary. This automatically runs the first option.

If no option is set, the routine simply checks that the files are stored safely.

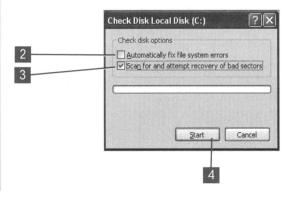

When you first start to write data onto a disk, the files are stored one after the other, with each occupying a continuous run of disk space. When you access one of these files, the drive simply finds the start point, then reads the data in a single sweep.

After the disk has been in use for some time, holes begin to appear in the layout, and not all files are stored in a continuous area. Some have been deleted, others will have grown during editing, so that they no longer fit in their original slot, but now have parts stored elsewhere on the disk. When you store a new file, there may not be a single space large enough for it, and it is stored in scattered sections. The drive is becoming *fragmented*. The data is still safe, but the access speed will suffer as the drive now has to hunt for each fragment of the file.

Disk Defragmenter should be run from time to time to pull scattered files together, so that they are stored in continuous blocks.

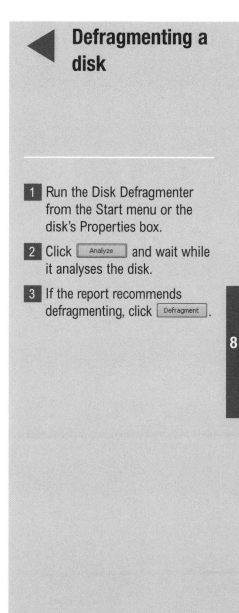

Defragmenting a disk

1. Run the Disk Defragmenter from the Start menu or the disk's Properties box.

2. Click [Analyze] and wait while it analyses the disk.

3. If the report recommends defragmenting, click [Defragment].

8

Backing up

If program files are accidentally deleted, it is a nuisance but not a major problem as you can reinstall the application from the original disks. Data files are different. How much is your data worth to you? How long would it take you to rewrite that report or re-edit that image? Individual files can be copied onto floppies for safekeeping, but if you have more than one or two it is simpler to use Backup. A backup job is easily set up and will more than pay for itself in time and effort if you ever need it!

Backups can be done on floppy disks. This is fine for home use or in a small business where there's not a lot to backup – with compression, over 2Mb of data will fit on one disk. If you intend to backup large quantities of data regularly, invest £100 or so in a tape drive so you don't have to struggle with a pile of floppies.

Advanced Backup settings

These can be set through the Advanced button on the summary panel. The main option is the *Type of Backup*:

- Normal, copies all the selected files and marks them as backed up.
- Copy, copies all the selected files, but without marking them as backed up.
- Incremental saves only those changed since last the Normal backup.
- Differential also saves only changed files, but without marking them as backed up.
- Daily saves only files created on the current day.

You can also specify the nature, placing and – most usefully – *scheduling*. If you are using a backup tape or other high capacity media, it makes sense to run the backup at non-working times.

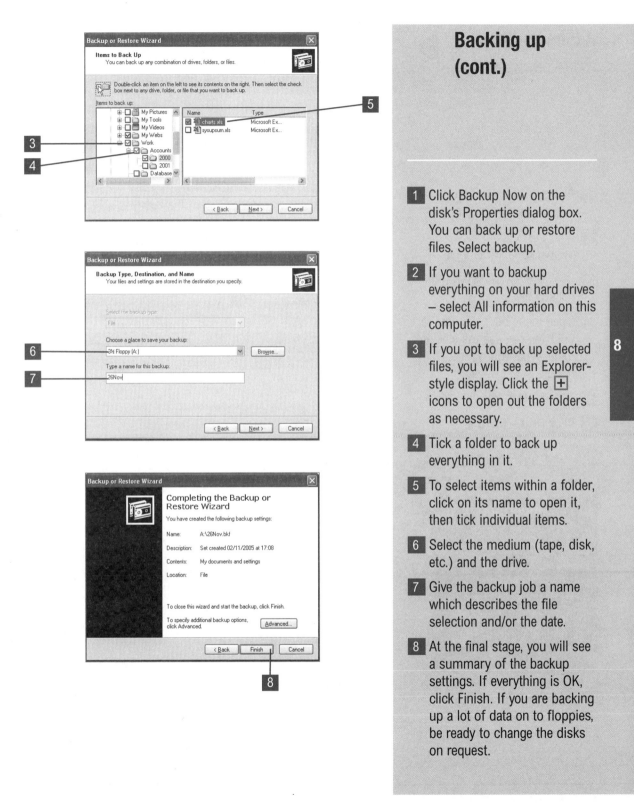

Backing up (cont.)

1. Click Backup Now on the disk's Properties dialog box. You can back up or restore files. Select backup.

2. If you want to backup everything on your hard drives – select All information on this computer.

3. If you opt to back up selected files, you will see an Explorer-style display. Click the ⊞ icons to open out the folders as necessary.

4. Tick a folder to back up everything in it.

5. To select items within a folder, click on its name to open it, then tick individual items.

6. Select the medium (tape, disk, etc.) and the drive.

7. Give the backup job a name which describes the file selection and/or the date.

8. At the final stage, you will see a summary of the backup settings. If everything is OK, click Finish. If you are backing up a lot of data on to floppies, be ready to change the disks on request.

Restoring files from backups ▶

With any luck this will never be necessary! But it's not difficult to do in any case. All you need to do is select the files that you want to restore, and let the wizard get on with it!

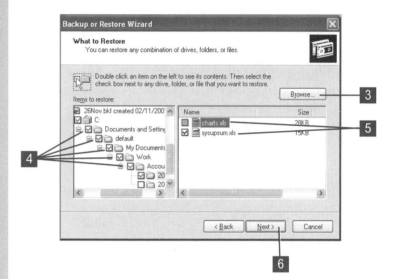

1. Run Backup, and select Restore at the opening panel.

2. Insert the disk or tape with the backup into its drive.

3. Click Browse and select the backup file.

4. Open the folders as necessary until you can see the files and folders that you want to restore.

5. Tick the files to select them.

6. Click Next – that's it.

Important !

There is an Advanced dialogue box where you set the type, schedule or other options. At some point, click the Advanced button and explore what's there.

Disk Cleanup is a neat little utility, and well worth running regularly – especially if you spend much time on the internet. When you are surfing, your browser stores the files for the text, graphics and programs on the web pages that you visit. This makes sense, as it means that if you go back to a page (either in the same session or at a later date), the browser can redraw it from the files, rather than having to download the whole lot again. However, if you don't revisit sites much, you can build up a lot of unwanted clutter on your disk. You can empty this cache from within your browser, but Cleanup will also do it.

The Recycle Bin can be emptied directly, or as part of the Cleanup.

Programs often create temporary files, but do not always remove them. Cleanup will also tidy up after them.

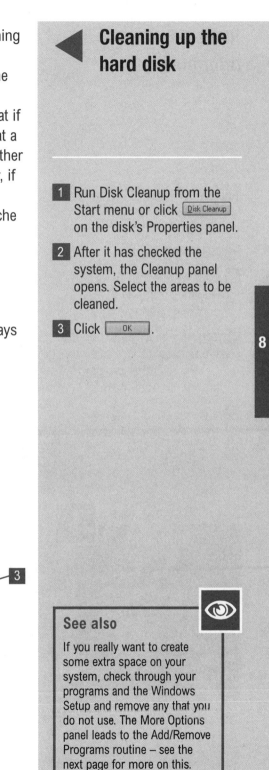

Cleaning up the hard disk

1 Run Disk Cleanup from the Start menu or click [Disk Cleanup] on the disk's Properties panel.

2 After it has checked the system, the Cleanup panel opens. Select the areas to be cleaned.

3 Click [OK].

8

See also

If you really want to create some extra space on your system, check through your programs and the Windows Setup and remove any that you do not use. The More Options panel leads to the Add/Remove Programs routine – see the next page for more on this.

Removing programs

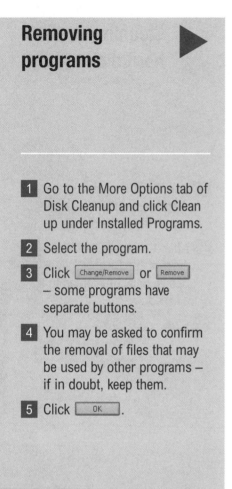

1 Go to the More Options tab of Disk Cleanup and click Clean up under Installed Programs.

2 Select the program.

3 Click `Change/Remove` or `Remove` – some programs have separate buttons.

4 You may be asked to confirm the removal of files that may be used by other programs – if in doubt, keep them.

5 Click `OK`.

Installing new applications is easy nowadays – you just put the CD in the drive and follow the instructions! Removing unused programs is also easy – but you must do it properly, and not simply delete the application's folder in Windows Explorer. When applications are installed, entries are created in the Start menu, and files are associated with them. These all need to be removed as well. The Remove Programs routine will take care of all of this for you.

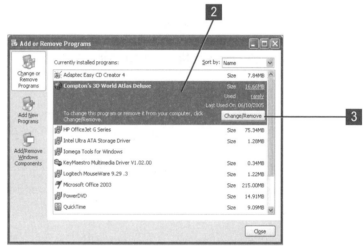

Important

If data files have been stored in the program's folder, the routine will not be able to remove them – use My Computer/Windows Explorer to tidy up any remnants.

Unwanted parts of Windows XP can also be removed – and you can add accessories that were omitted during the initial installation.

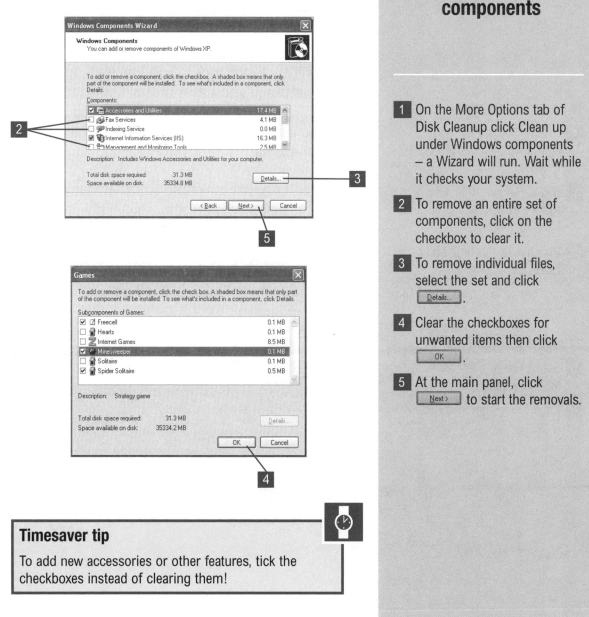

1. On the More Options tab of Disk Cleanup click Clean up under Windows components – a Wizard will run. Wait while it checks your system.

2. To remove an entire set of components, click on the checkbox to clear it.

3. To remove individual files, select the set and click Details... .

4. Clear the checkboxes for unwanted items then click OK .

5. At the main panel, click Next > to start the removals.

8

Timesaver tip

To add new accessories or other features, tick the checkboxes instead of clearing them!

Restoring your system

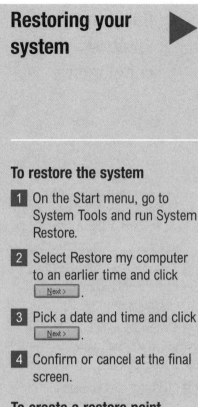

To restore the system

1. On the Start menu, go to System Tools and run System Restore.

2. Select Restore my computer to an earlier time and click `Next >`.

3. Pick a date and time and click `Next >`.

4. Confirm or cancel at the final screen.

To create a restore point

5. Select Create a restore point and click `Next >`.

6. Enter a description and click `Next >`.

You may never need to use System Restore – but if you do, you will be very glad that it was there! System Restore helps you to recover from disaster. It works by taking copies of your essential files at regular intervals – once or twice a day. If any of those files become corrupted or erased – accidentally or otherwise – System Restore will put things back to how they were. Just run the application and select a restore point when things were well – normally the previous day's, but you may need to go back further if there have been problems lurking for a while.

For extra security, you can create your own 'restore points' before installing new software. A badly-designed application may occasionally mess up existing settings.

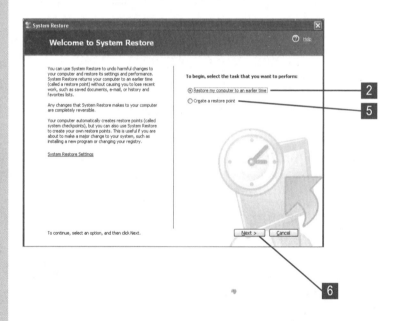

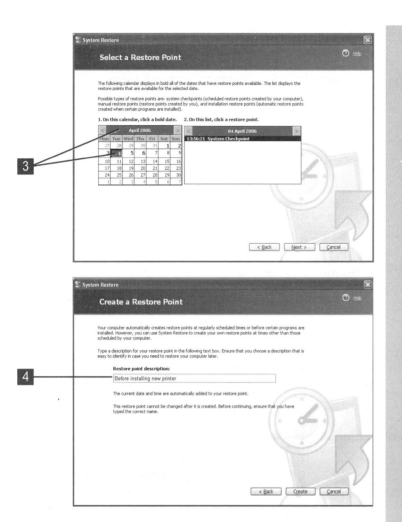

Did you know?

You do not have to set the time and date when creating a restore point because these are stamped on the restore point automatically.

Keeping Windows up-to-date

1. Run Internet Explorer.
2. Click the Windows Update link, or select it from the Links folder of the Favorites.
3. Wait while the Update Wizard scans your PC.
4. Scroll through, selecting the updates that you want.
5. Check the selection and click Install Now.
6. Wait while the software is downloaded and installed.

Microsoft regularly produces improvements and bug-fixes for Windows, distributing them through the internet. Windows has an Automatic Updates routine, which can connect regularly to Microsoft's site to get the latest patches and additions.

The Automatic Updates settings can be changed through the System Properties item in the Control Panel. It can:

- Download automatically, notifying you when the files are ready to be installed.
- Alert you if it finds any new critical or optional updates.
- Be turned off completely, if you prefer to use the Windows Update link to check the site when it suits you.

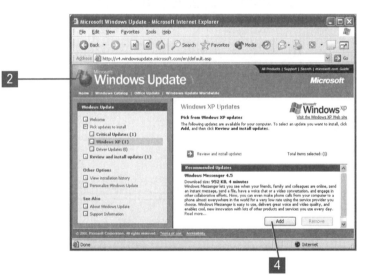

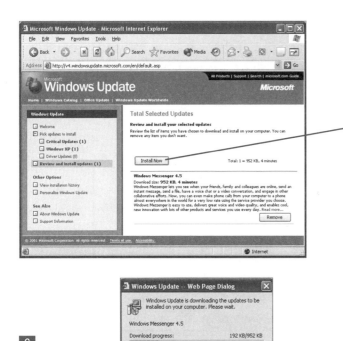

5

6

8

Important

After the files have been downloaded and installed, you normally have to restart the PC to bring them into play, but it doesn't have to be done immediately – finish your session as usual. At the next start up, there will probably be a delay while your system files are updated.

See also

See Chapter 9 to learn how to use Internet Explorer.

Adding a printer ▶

If your printer is not detected and installed automatically by the plug and play technology, you can add it yourself easily. There is a wizard to take you through the steps, and Windows XP has **drivers** for almost all but the most recent printers. If you have a *very* new machine, use the drivers on the printer's setup disk.

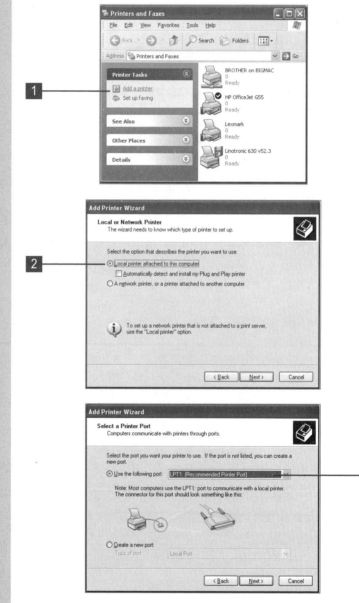

1 Click Add a printer in the Print Tasks set to start the wizard.

2 On a home machine, the printer is probably attached to your PC, so select Local.

3 Select the Port – normally LPT1.

either

4 Pick the Manufacturer then the Printer from the lists.

or

5 Insert a disk with the printer driver and click Have Disk.

6 Change the name if you like – a networked printer should have a clear recognisable name to identify it.

7 Set the printer as the default if appropriate.

8 At the final stage opt for the test print, then click Finish and wait.

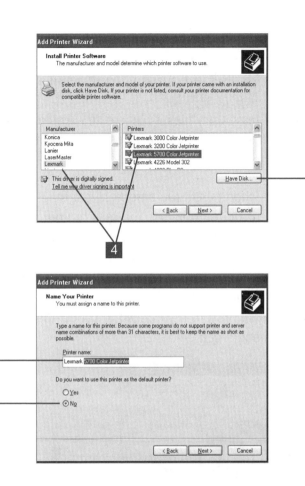

8

Jargon buster

Drivers – software that converts the formatting information from an application into the right codes for the printer.

Cancelling a print job ▶

When you send a document for printing, Windows XP will happily handle it in the background. It prepares the file for the printer, stores it in a queue if the printer is already busy or off-line, pushes the pages out one at a time and deletes the temporary files it has created. Nothing visible happens on screen – unless the printer runs out of paper or has other faults.

This is fine when things run smoothly, but they don't always when you are printing. You may run out of ink or paper part way through the job; you may decide that you don't like the look of the first page of a long document so that there is no point in printing the rest; and sometimes your PC and your printer will get their wires crossed for no discernable reason. If you need to cancel the printing of a document, it can be done.

1 Open the Printers folder, right-click on the active printer and select Open.

or

2 Right-click on the 🖨 icon in the Taskbar and select the printer.

3 Select the file(s).

4 Press [Delete] or open the Document menu and select Cancel.

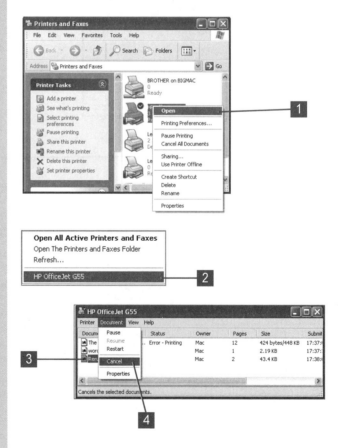

The internet

Introduction

This chapter aims to introduce some of the basic concepts of and ways of working on the internet, and explore just a few of its almost infinite possibilities. I've tried to keep things as simple as possible, which hasn't been that difficult for me because the key internet activities are essentially quite simple. There are all sorts of refinements and alternative ways of achieving similar results, and there are a few complexities, but these can be ignored until you are ready to deal with them. Of course, this simplified approach does mean that if things go wrong – and they do from time to time – you may not know how to deal with it. But let's be positive. As long as you follow the instructions, you should be fine, and an hour or so from now, you should have visited dozens of websites and found out all sorts of interesting things.

The software that is used here is Internet Explorer. This is supplied as part of Windows, and is a powerful piece of software – easy to use but with all the sophisticated features that you need to get the best out of browsing the World Wide Web. Only the main features are covered here, but that is all you need to get started. The screenshots are from Internet Explorer 6.0, the latest version at the time of writing. If you have an earlier version, you should not find many significant differences (as long as yours is no older than 4.0) – the newer versions have a few extra features, but the main menu commands, tools and options are exactly the same. If you have a later version, then I hope that things haven't changed much!

To use this chapter, you need to have an internet connection already in place, or if you haven't got one of your own yet, you need to visit one of the kids or a friend, or go to the public library – somewhere that you can get online.

Jargon buster

Browser – application specially designed for accessing and displaying the information in the World Wide Web. This is also true the other way: the web is an information system designed to be viewed on browsers.

Email – electronic mail, a system for sending messages and files across networks.

HTML – HyperText Markup Language, a system of instructions that browsers can interpret to display text and images. HTML allows hypertext links to be built into web pages.

Net – short for internet. And internet is short for interlinked networks, which is what it is. (See Chapter 2 for more details.)

Page – or web page, a document displayed on the web. It may be plain or formatted text; and may hold pictures, sounds   and videos.

Web – World Wide Web. Also shortened to WWW or W3.

Let's start by clearing up a common misconception. The 'web' and the 'internet' are not the same thing. Some people use the terms interchangeably, but they shouldn't.

- The **internet** is the underlying framework. It consists of the computers, large and small, that store and process information for the internet; the telephone wire, network cable, microwave links and other connections between them; and the software systems that allow them all to interact.
- The **World Wide Web** is the most visible and one of the simplest and most popular ways of using the net. It consists of – literally – billions of web **pages**, which can be viewed through browsers, such as Internet Explorer. The pages are constructed using **HTML**, that tells **browsers** how to display text and images, and how to manage links between pages. Clicking on a hypertext link in a page tells the browser to go to the linked page (or sometimes to a different type of linked file) – wherever it may be.

Email is another simple and very popular use of the internet, and there are other more specialised internet activities, as you will see later in this book.

◀ **Discovering the internet and the web**

9

Starting to browse ▶

1 Click the Internet Explorer item at the top of the Start menu.

    or

2 Double-click the Internet Explorer icon on the Desktop.

3 Wait a few moments for Internet Explorer to start.

4 If Internet Explorer is set to connect to a website when it first starts, then the Connection dialogue box will appear automatically. If it does not, double-click the desktop icon for your internet connection (Mine is Speedtouch, yours may well be different.)

5 The Connection dialogue box will have the User name already in place. The Password may also be there; if not type it in now.

6 Click ⬚Connect.

7 Wait a few seconds.

Without further ado, let's go online and browse the World Wide Web. To do this you must first start Internet Explorer and connect to your internet service provider.

You may find that when you start Internet Explorer, it will automatically try to make the connection. You may have to start the program and make the connection as two separate jobs. It all depends on your PC's setup – but either way, there's nothing difficult here, once you have located the icons on the Desktop or the Start menu.

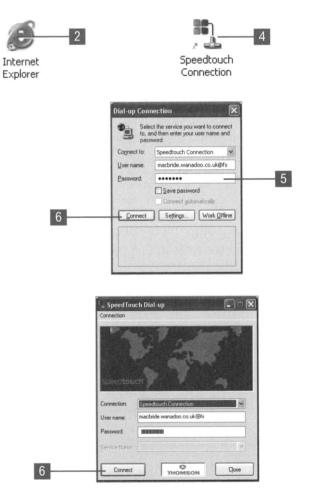

Internet Explorer

Speedtouch Connection

We had a quick look at the Internet Explorer window in
Chapter 1, but concentrated on the absolute essentials.
Let's have a closer look at the display, and take in more of
its features.

Menu bar

Standard toolbar

Address bar

Links toolbar

Explorer bar

Divider

Hand pointer –
appears when
you point to a link

Title bar   Go button

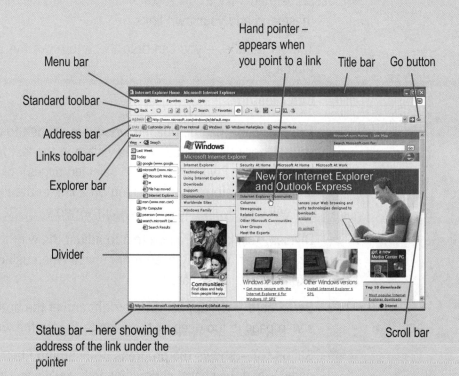

Status bar – here showing the
address of the link under the
pointer

Scroll bar

Discovering Internet Explorer (cont.)

The toolbars

Title bar – shows the title of the Web page, which is not the same as its URL.

Menu bar – gives you access to the full set of commands.

Standard toolbar – with tools for the most commonly-used commands.

This and the Address and Links bars can be hidden if not wanted.

Address bar – shows the URL (Uniform Resource Locator, the address and filename) of the page. Addresses can be typed here.

Go button – click after typing an URL in the Address bar.

Links toolbar – links to selected sites. There are predefined links to Microsoft's sites, but you can change these and add your own links.

Toolbar handles – you can drag these to move the toolbars.

Other features

Explorer bar – can be opened when it is needed to display your History (links to the places visited in the last few days) or your Favorites (links to selected pages), or to run a search for information. Clicking on a link in the Explorer bar will display its page in the main window.

Divider – click and drag on this to adjust the width of the Explorer bar. You may need more space when using the Explorer bar for a search.

Scroll bars – will appear on the right and at the bottom if a web page is too deep or too wide to fit into the window.

Status bar – shows the progress of incoming files for a page. When they have all downloaded, you'll see 'Done'. It also shows the address in a link when you point to it.

Exploring the standard toolbar

This can be customised – you can choose which tools to include, and how to display them (page 85). Almost all of the basic set of tools are shown here.

If you have Microsoft Office installed, this will have added a couple of extra tools.

(page 85)

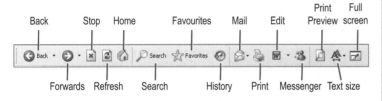

Back takes you to the last page visited. The arrow to its right opens a drop-down list showing last half dozen or so pages – click on one to jump directly back to it.

Once you have gone back, Forward becomes active, and the visited pages are added to its list.

Stop stops downloading the current page.

Refresh reloads the current page.

Home will take you back to the place you have designated as the home page.

Search, Favourites and History open, or close if already open, their displays in the Explorer Bar.

Clicking the Mail button opens a drop-down list with a set of commands for handling email.

Print sends the current page to the printer, using the default settings.

The Edit button takes the current page into your default editor. The arrow opens a drop-down list of the editors on your PC.

Discovering Internet Explorer (cont.)

See also

See 'Using Favorites' on page 239 and 'Viewing the History list' on page 243 for more on these uses of the Explorer bar.

See 'Printing web pages' on page 247 to find out about the Print options.

Timesaver tip

If you are having trouble downloading a web page, it may help to start again from scratch. Click Stop, then Refresh.

Messenger runs Windows Messenger.

Print Preview shows how the printed page will look – this may be different from the screen display.

Text size lets you change the size of the text.

Full screen expands the display to fill the screen and hides everything except the standard toolbar and the page itself. Click it again to return to the normal layout.

If you want to 'browse' the web, all you need is a good place to start, and one of the best places is a net directory – a site with sets of organised links to other sites. And one of the best directories is Yahoo! UK. (This is the UK branch of a world-wide web service – the original Yahoo! is US-based, and there is a local Yahoo! in many countries.) What makes it so useful is that it is extremely comprehensive, but all the sites listed there have been recommended by someone at some point. Quality control is rare on the web.

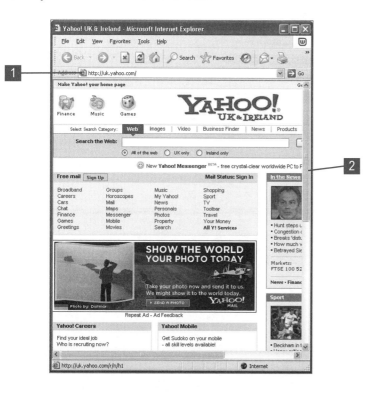

Browsing the web

1 Go to Yahoo! UK by typing this address into the Address bar: **uk.yahoo.com**

2 There's lots of stuff on the entry page at Yahoo! At the top you will see links to its many services, plus news and sports headlines. Ignore all these for now, as we want the directory. Use the scroll bar to go down to the bottom of the page.

3 Think of a topic that interests you and in the web directory area click on the heading that the topic would fall under.

9

Browsing the
web (cont.)

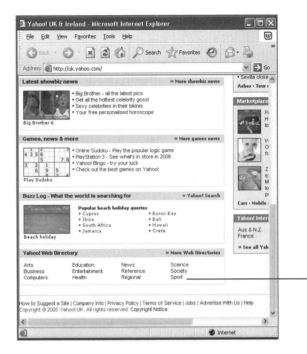

! Important

A hyperlink (link for short) is a connection to another web page. When you click on a link, Internet Explorer goes to that page and displays it. You know when you are on a link because the ⇖ pointer becomes a ⤵ hand.

When you are looking for material at Yahoo! don't worry too much if you are not sure which category your topic will fit into. The directory is so well cross-referenced that any reasonable start point should get you there.

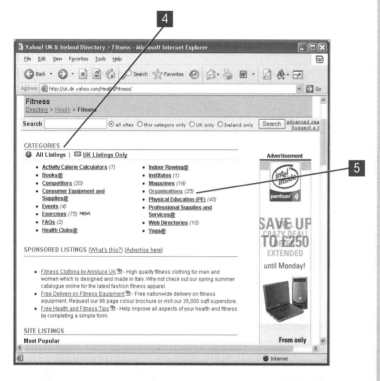

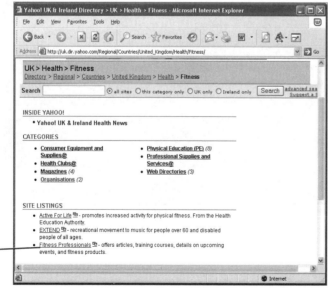

4 The directory is organised as a hierarchy with many levels. At each level there are three sets of links.

At the top are links to Categories – most of these are subdivisions of the current category; those with @ after the name are cross-links to other parts of the hierarchy.

The second set are Sponsored links – i.e. to firms that have paid to be included.

The third set are the Site listings.

As you work down through the levels, the first set shrinks, and the third set grows.

5 Use the category links to get down through two or three levels, to reach a specialised topic of your choice.

6 Click a Site listing link.

9

Browsing the web (cont.)

There's so much to see on the web! In fact, there's too much. You can often find links to scores – or even hundreds – of sites on a topic, so you have to learn to be selective or you can waste an awful lot of time online. Dip into a site to get an idea of what it is like, and if this is not really what you are looking for, move on and try elsewhere.

7 When the new page has loaded in, read to see if it is of interest. If you see a link that looks promising, click on it to find out where it leads.

8 If you want to go back to the previous page at the site, or back from there to Yahoo!, click [◀ Back ▾].

9 If you want to start browsing a new topic, either work your way back to the start page in Yahoo!, or enter the uk.yahoo.com address and start again from the top.

Important

Sometimes when you click on a link, the new page opens in a new window. This can be useful as it means that the previous page is still there in the original Internet Explorer window. However, there are a couple of catches. It can get a bit confusing if you have too many windows open at once, and the Back button only works within the same window. As a general rule, if a site has opened in a new window, close the window when you have finished with that site.

Web directories offer one approach to finding material on the web. Search engines offer another, and this is often the best way if you are looking for very specific information. A search engine is a site that has compiled an index to web pages, and which lets you search through the index. There are several dozen search engines, and they compile their indices in different ways and to different levels of completeness, but some of the best know what's on 80% or more of the pages on the web. The most complete and the most effective is Google. It is so well used and loved that searching the web is now often called 'googling'.

You search by giving one or more words to specify what you are looking for. Try to be specific. If you search for 'football', 'bridge' or 'gardening' you will get millions of links to possible pages.

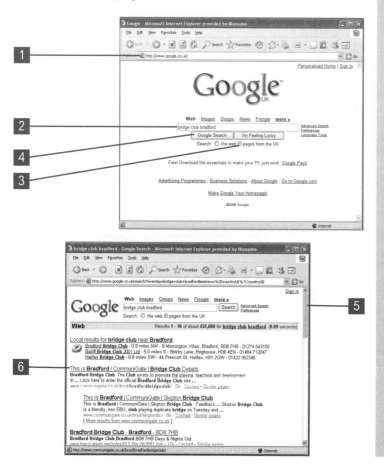

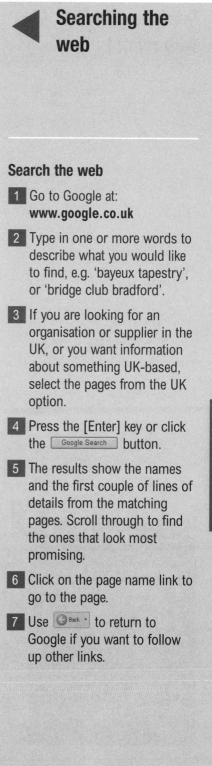

Searching the web

Search the web

1 Go to Google at:
www.google.co.uk

2 Type in one or more words to describe what you would like to find, e.g. 'bayeux tapestry', or 'bridge club bradford'.

3 If you are looking for an organisation or supplier in the UK, or you want information about something UK-based, select the pages from the UK option.

4 Press the [Enter] key or click the [Google Search] button.

5 The results show the names and the first couple of lines of details from the matching pages. Scroll through to find the ones that look most promising.

6 Click on the page name link to go to the page.

7 Use [Back] to return to Google if you want to follow up other links.

9

Searching the web (cont.)

Google has links to over 8 billion pages in its index! Which is why you have to be as specific as possible when looking for particular information. However, sometimes it pays to be less specific, as this can produce leads that you might never have thought of yourself.

It doesn't matter too much if you get millions of results from a search as the good stuff tends to be listed at the top. (Google has developed some very clever systems for rating pages.)

! Important

You will find a link to the next page at the bottom of the results listing, but as a general rule, if you don't see anything useful in the first page, subsequent pages are unlikely to be any better. Try a new search, with different words.

A favourite is an address stored in an easily-managed list. To return to a favourite place, you simply click on it in the list.

Favourites can be accessed through the Favourites menu or through the Explorer bar. We'll start with the menu approach.

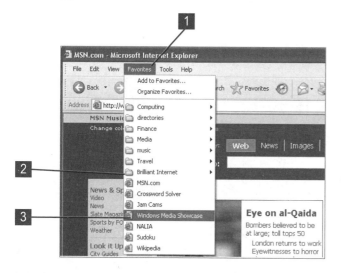

Using Favourites

1 Open the Favourites menu.

2 If the Favourite is in a folder, open its sub-menu.

3 Click on the one you want.

Did you know?

Even if you haven't yet added a Favourite of your own, there should be some already in the list – mainly to Microsoft's sites.

9

Adding a favourite ▶

Addresses are a pain to type. One mistake and either you don't get there at all, or you find yourself at a totally unexpected site. (Try www.microsfot.com sometime.) Favourites are one way of being able to return to a site without having to retype its address.

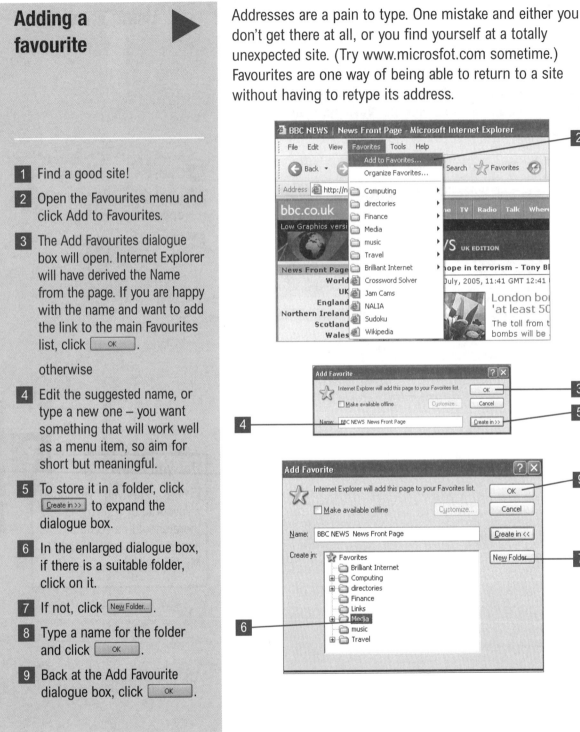

1 Find a good site!

2 Open the Favourites menu and click Add to Favourites.

3 The Add Favourites dialogue box will open. Internet Explorer will have derived the Name from the page. If you are happy with the name and want to add the link to the main Favourites list, click ⌷ OK ⌷.

otherwise

4 Edit the suggested name, or type a new one – you want something that will work well as a menu item, so aim for short but meaningful.

5 To store it in a folder, click ⌷ Create in >> ⌷ to expand the dialogue box.

6 In the enlarged dialogue box, if there is a suitable folder, click on it.

7 If not, click ⌷ New Folder... ⌷.

8 Type a name for the folder and click ⌷ OK ⌷.

9 Back at the Add Favourite dialogue box, click ⌷ OK ⌷.

You can store your favourites in one simple list, but this soon gets unwieldy. If there are more than about twenty items, the menu takes up too much screen space and it can be hard to find the favourite you want. The solution is to organise your favourites into folders, which then become sub-menus in the Favourites system. It's easy to create new folders and to move entries into them.

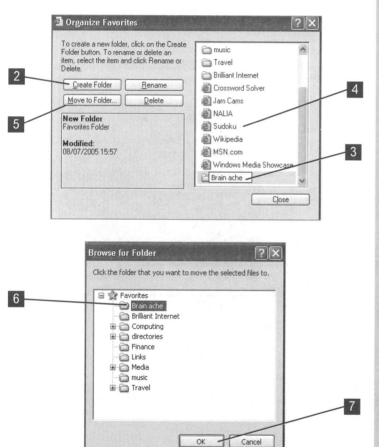

◀ Organising your Favourites

1 Click Organise Favourites on the Favourites menu.

2 Click [Create Folder].

3 A new folder will appear. Give it a suitable name.

4 Drag the link on to the folder and drop it in. If you pause over the folder first, it will open and you can then place the link exactly where you want it in the list.

or

5 Select the link and click [Move to Folder...].

6 Select the folder from the list.

7 Click [OK].

9

Using History

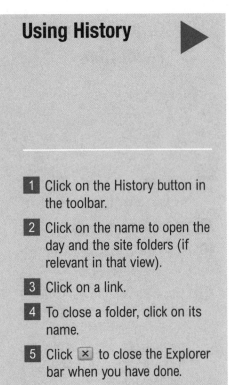

As you browse, each page is recorded in the History list as an internet shortcut – i.e. a link to the page. Clicking the History button opens the History list in the Explorer bar. Click a link from here to go to the page.

If you are online at the time, Internet Explorer will connect to the page. If you are offline, it will display the page if all the necessary files are still available in the temporary internet files folder, otherwise it will ask you to connect.

1. Click on the History button in the toolbar.

2. Click on the name to open the day and the site folders (if relevant in that view).

3. Click on a link.

4. To close a folder, click on its name.

5. Click ☒ to close the Explorer bar when you have done.

The History list can be viewed in four ways:

- By Date groups the links into folders by date and then by site. This is useful if you know when you were last there, but not the name of the site – and you may well not know where a page was if you reached it through a hyperlink.
- By Site groups the links into folders by site. This is probably the most convenient view most of the time.
- By Most Visited lists individual page links in the order that you visit them most. If there are search engines or directories that you regularly use as start points for browsing sessions, they will be up at the top of the list.
- By Order Visited Today lists the individual pages in simple time order. Use this view to backtrack past the links that are stored in the drop-down list of the Back button.

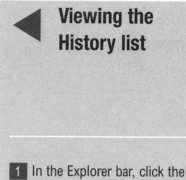

Viewing the History list

1 In the Explorer bar, click the View button to open the View menu.

2 Select the view which you think will enable you to find the required page fastest.

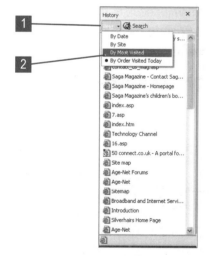

9

Timesaver tip

If the History list starts to get clogged up, you can delete sites or individual pages within sites. Right-click on the site or page and select Delete from the pop-up menu that appears.

Managing temporary internet files

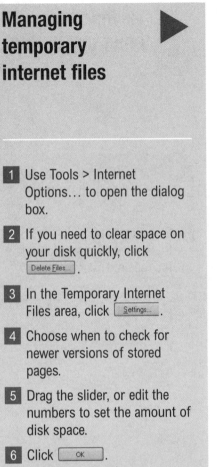

1. Use Tools > Internet Options… to open the dialog box.

2. If you need to clear space on your disk quickly, click `Delete Files…`.

3. In the Temporary Internet Files area, click `Settings…`.

4. Choose when to check for newer versions of stored pages.

5. Drag the slider, or edit the numbers to set the amount of disk space.

6. Click `OK`.

When you visit a web page, the files that create it are downloaded onto your PC. These files are retained, and if you return to that page, either during the same session or later, it will then use the stored files, which is quicker than downloading them again. It also means that you can revisit pages offline.

You can set the amount of storage space to suit the way you surf and the size of your hard disk. If you have plenty of space and you tend to go back to sites a lot – perhaps following up a succession of links from one start point, or perhaps because you like to revisit sites offline – give yourself a big cache. If space is a problem, cut the cache right down. And if you need to free up the disk space, delete all the stored files.

You can also choose when Internet Explorer should check for newer versions of the stored pages. The 'Automatically' setting should do the job – this will check at the first visit in a session, but select the 'Every visit to the page' option if your favourite sites are fast-changing ones, e.g. news sites.

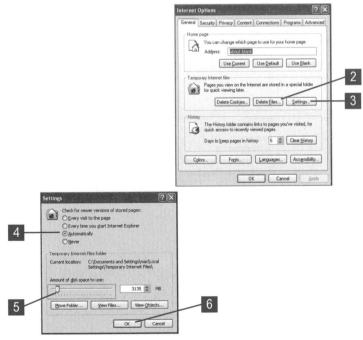

If you visit a lot of sites during your online sessions, and/or have set the number of days to keep the History links to a high value, then your History list could get very long. Beyond a certain point, its value as an aid to better browsing starts to diminish. You are probably best to set the days to no more than seven. The situations in which the History is most useful are those where you want to look back in leisurely offline time at pages that you glanced at while online, and you are most likely to do that either on the same day or within a couple of days. When you find sites that you will want to return to regularly, don't use the History – add them to your Favourites.

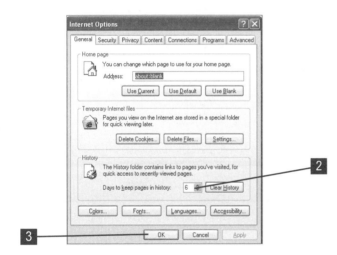

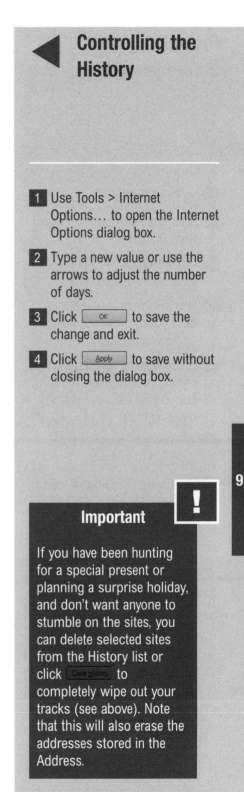

1 Use Tools > Internet Options... to open the Internet Options dialog box.

2 Type a new value or use the arrows to adjust the number of days.

3 Click ⎡ OK ⎤ to save the change and exit.

4 Click ⎡ Apply ⎤ to save without closing the dialog box.

9

❗ Important

If you have been hunting for a special present or planning a surprise holiday, and don't want anyone to stumble on the sites, you can delete selected sites from the History list or click ⎡ Clear History ⎤ to completely wipe out your tracks (see above). Note that this will also erase the addresses stored in the Address.

Previewing before you print

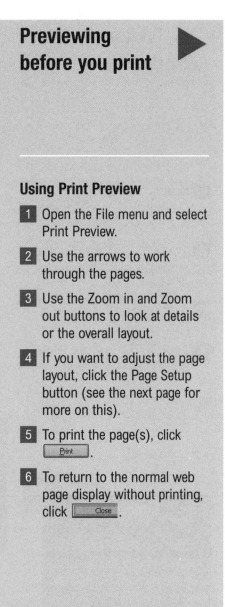

Using Print Preview

1. Open the File menu and select Print Preview.

2. Use the arrows to work through the pages.

3. Use the Zoom in and Zoom out buttons to look at details or the overall layout.

4. If you want to adjust the page layout, click the Page Setup button (see the next page for more on this).

5. To print the page(s), click Print .

6. To return to the normal web page display without printing, click Close .

A sheet of A4 paper and a computer screen are rather different shapes, and pages can be laid out on the screen in different ways. What this means is that you can never be entirely sure what a web page will look like when it is printed, or how many sheets it will be printed on – unless you use Print Preview. If the preview is acceptable, you can send it straight to the printer; if adjusting the layout might give a better printout, you can open the Page Setup dialogue box and change the settings.

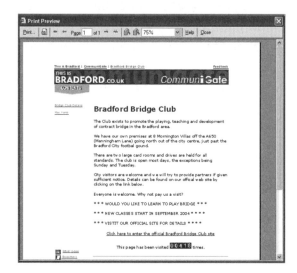

If you just want a printed copy of the whole of the current page, you simply click the Print button. Sometimes you need to control the printout – you may only want part of a long page or a section of a framed page, or you may want to print sideways on the paper (landscape orientation), or print several copies. In these cases, you need to go into the Print dialogue box.

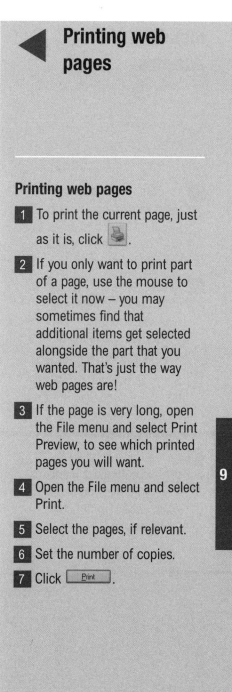

Timesaver tip

You can sometimes get better results by copying part or all of a page into your word processor and printing it from there.

Printing web pages

Printing web pages

1 To print the current page, just as it is, click 🖨.

2 If you only want to print part of a page, use the mouse to select it now – you may sometimes find that additional items get selected alongside the part that you wanted. That's just the way web pages are!

3 If the page is very long, open the File menu and select Print Preview, to see which printed pages you will want.

4 Open the File menu and select Print.

5 Select the pages, if relevant.

6 Set the number of copies.

7 Click ⬚ Print ⬚.

9

The internet 247

Installing add-ons ▶

Browsers can display only formatted text and GIF and JPG graphics; but add-ons extend the range of files that they can handle. These are extensions to the browser, not independent applications. Some are present from the start, others can be downloaded from Microsoft or other sources when they are needed. Whenever you meet a file that needs an add-on, it will normally be accompanied by a link that you can use to get the software. Exactly what you have to do to download and install the add-on varies, though the process is almost always straightforward and there are usually clear instructions. Here, for example, is what happens when you install RealPlayer.

1 You will be alerted when you need an add-on, and you will be offered a link to a site from whence you can download it. Follow the link.

2 At the site, read the instructions. If there are different versions of the software, choose the one for your computer system.

3 Start the download. You will be asked if you want to run or save the software. Click Save .

4 Pick a folder to store the file – use My Documents or any folder that you can find again easily. Do not change the filename!

Installing add-ons (cont.)

5 Wait while the file downloads. If you have a normal (56k) phone connection, this could take a while!

6 Installation may start automatically. If it does not, go to the folder in Windows Explorer or My Computer and double-click on the file to start the installer.

7 You will be asked if to confirm the installation. Click ⬚ Install ⬚.

8 You may be asked to configure the software to your system. Set the options to suit, leaving at their defaults any that you do not understand.

9

Did you know?

Add-ons are almost always free. Their manufacturers make money by charging for the applications that create the files that the add-ons play.

Getting Adobe Reader ▶

Adobe Reader is one add-on that you really should have, as it is what you need to view and print PDF documents. People use PDFs for booklets and brochures, for books (this one went to the printer's as a PDF) and for paper sculpture kits (see the Did you know?) – in fact, for any document where well-formatted text and images are needed. PDF stands for Portable Document Format, and it is portable. A PDF file can be viewed on any computer or printed on any printer and the result will be the same.

1 When you try to open or download a PDF file you should find a link to get the Adobe Reader 'Plug-in'. Click it.

or

2 Head directly to Adobe at **www.adobe.com** and follow the links to get the Reader.

3 Follow the instructions to Download and install the Reader.

4 When you next come across a PDF file, Reader will start up inside Internet Explorer. Use its toolbar buttons to save, print or do other work with the document.

? Did you know?

Yamaha Motor Company have some lovely paper model kits (in PDFs) for free downloading – great for the grandkids on rainy afternoons! Find them at **www.yamaha-motor.co.jp**. Follow the links to Entertainment and then Paper Craft.

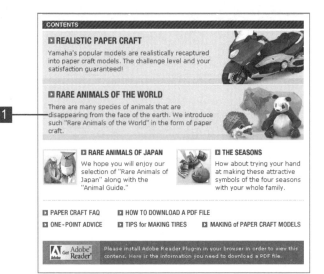

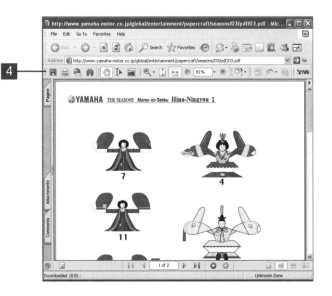

With a broadband connection, it costs you nothing to leave the line open all the time that you are at the computer – so that you can pick up or send mail, or look something up on the web whenever you want. You only need to end the connection when you close down the computer.

With a standard dial-up connection, it is a different matter altogether. When you are online you may be paying for the cost of the phone call (or not, it depends upon the nature of your service contract) but you are certainly tying up the telephone line. You should end the connection as soon as you have finished working online.

You should close the connection properly – don't just close the browser or Outlook Express. This ensures that you are properly disconnected from your service provider's computer.

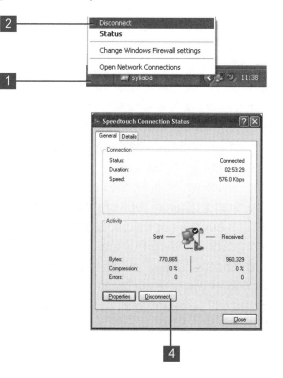

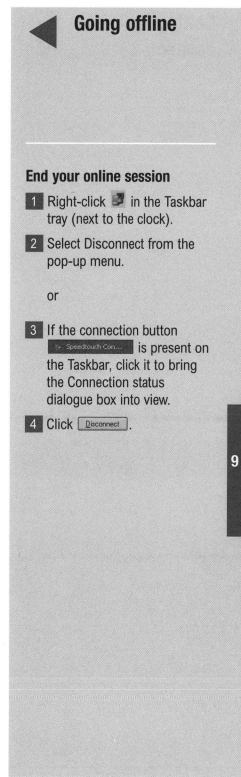

Going offline

End your online session

1 Right-click 🖳 in the Taskbar tray (next to the clock).

2 Select Disconnect from the pop-up menu.

or

3 If the connection button ⟨ Speedtouch Con... ⟩ is present on the Taskbar, click it to bring the Connection status dialogue box into view.

4 Click ⟨ Disconnect ⟩.

9

Getting connected ▶

Some of you may have been working on someone else's connection while reading this chapter, so before we leave, let's have a look at how to get connected. It's not hard. When I first went online, in the late 1980s, getting connected required relatively expensive equipment and quite a lot of technical know-how – and there wasn't that much to do once you got online! Today, the costs are minimal, no technical knowledge is needed, and the online possibilities are amazing.

To get connected you need four things:

■ A computer – any reasonably modern computer will do. It does not need to be state-of-the-art or top-of-the-range. If you are buying a new system, the cheapest Windows XP PC will do the job, or even a second-hand Windows 98 machine – as long as it is in good condition. Apple Macs are fine, and less susceptible to viruses (which are mainly written by Windows programmers), but they are more expensive to buy and there is less software available for Apples. Cost: under £400 for a desktop PC complete with Windows, Internet Explorer, Outlook Express, a word processor, and other entry-level but adequate software. Spend more only if you need a higher specification machine, or more sophisticated software for other uses.

■ A modem – the device which links the computer to the phone line. You need a different type of modem for a dial-up connection down a normal phone line than for a broadband connection. Modern PCs are usually sold with a standard modem built-in, and so are ready for a dial-up connection. If you take the broadband alternative, a suitable modem will be supplied as part of the deal.

■ A phone line – or more to the point, a phone socket within reach of the computer. If necessary, you can get extension phone leads at any good DIY store. Cost: £5–£10.

- An account with an internet service provider – the company that will link you to the internet and provide you with your email address and web space if you want to set up a site.

How do I choose an ISP?

There are basically three types of ISP account.

- A broadband connection gives high-speed access to the internet. This uses the normal phone line, but the line has to be reconfigured at the exchange before it can be used. Not all local exchanges have this capacity, so the first thing to do is to check that broadband is available in your area. Broadband users can connect at the start of the day and leave it connected until they shut down – it costs nothing and causes no problems as the phone can be used for normal calls while the computer is online.

There are several variables: speed, download limits, number of email addresses that you can run from one account, and whether or not you are given web space. The cost will vary to match, from around £15 to £30 a month. You only need the very high speeds and high download limits if you intend to download a lot of music or videos. All broadband ISPs offer a free modem, but you must sign up for a minimum of 1 year.

Broadband providers include AOL, Wanadoo, BTInternet, NTL and most other phone companies.

- A monthly contract dial-up account. This will work on any phone line – you can even connect through a mobile if you have a suitable lead. Though far slower than broadband, dial-up is what we all managed with perfectly happily until recently. Expect to pay £15 a month, and to get unlimited access on an 0800 line.

Getting connected (cont.)

■ A pay-as-you-go dial-up account. These also run on the standard phone line. They typically cost 1p per minute, with the charging done through your phone bill as the connections are to 0844 or 0845 number. If you mainly use the internet for email, with occasional dips into the web to look things up, then pay-as-you-go can be an economic solution – one brief phone call a day to collect and receive your email should add up to a little over £1 a month. Dial-up account providers include AOL, Wanadoo and many smaller firms, including my own excellent TCP.

The problem is, you don't really know what you need until you have been active online for a while. So here's a suggestion. Several ISPs – notably AOL – offer a free month's trial of their dial-up service. Try it. See how you get on, and make an informed decision at the end of the month.

Email

Introduction

The World Wide Web may well be the most glamorous aspect of the internet and the one that grabs newcomers, but email is the aspect that many people find the most useful in the long run. It is quick, reliable and simple to use.

■ Email is quick. When you send a message to someone, it will normally reach their mailbox within minutes – and usually within half an hour. However, it will only be read when the recipient collects the mail, and that may be anything from a few minutes later to when they get back from holiday.

■ Email is reliable. As long as you have the address right, the message is almost certain to get through. And on those rare occasions when it doesn't, you will usually get it back with an 'undeliverable' note attached.

■ Email is simple to use. You can learn the essential skills in minutes – as you will see very shortly!

What you'll do

Understand email

Start Outlook Express

Explore the toolbar

Read an email message

Add an address to the Address Book

Find a contact

Write a message

Reply to an email

Forward a message

Attach a file to a message

Save an attached file

Open an attachment

Adjust the layout

Control the Preview pane

Understanding email ▶

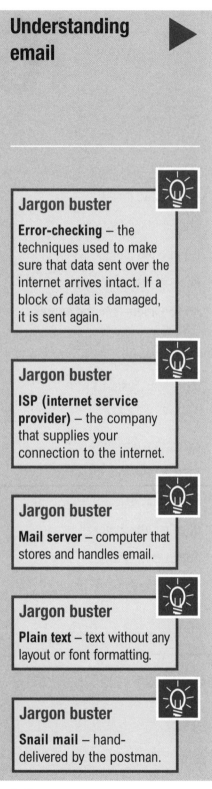

Jargon buster

Error-checking – the techniques used to make sure that data sent over the internet arrives intact. If a block of data is damaged, it is sent again.

Jargon buster

ISP (internet service provider) – the company that supplies your connection to the internet.

Jargon buster

Mail server – computer that stores and handles email.

Jargon buster

Plain text – text without any layout or font formatting.

Jargon buster

Snail mail – hand-delivered by the postman.

It may help you to have an overview of the technology behind email, so you can use it more efficiently and are less likely to get fazed when things don't quite go according to plan!

When you send an email message, it does not go direct to your recipient, as a phone call does. Instead it will travel through perhaps a dozen or more computers before arriving at its destination – in the same way that **snail mail** passes through several post offices and depots. The message goes first to the **mail server** at your **ISP**. This will work out which computer to send it to, to help it towards its destination. The server will normally hold the message briefly, while it assembles a handful of messages to send to the next place – in the same way that the Post Office sorts and bags its mail. Each mail server along the way will do the same thing, bundling the message with others heading in the same direction. This method gives more efficient internet traffic and at the cost of very little delay – most messages will normally be delivered in less than an hour.

However, your recipients won't necessarily be reading the message within the hour. The delivery is to their mail boxes at their service providers. People only get their email when they go online to collect it. (Though with a broadband account and automated collection it can feel as if its delivered.)

Email messages are sent as text files. A **plain text** message will normally be very short, as it takes only one byte to represent a character – (plus about 10% more for **error-checking**). A ten-line message, for example, will make a file of around 1 Kb, and that can be transmitted in about 3 seconds. Images, video clips and other files can be sent by mail (see page 270) but they must first be converted into text format. You don't need to worry about how this is done, as Outlook Express will do all the conversion automatically. What you do need to know is that conversion increases the size of files by around 50%, so even quite small images can significantly increase the time it takes to send or receive messages.

Outlook Express is currently the most widely used email software among private users. It is very simple to use – you can pick up your mail with one click of a button, and though it takes a little more to send a message, there's nothing complicated in it.

Views bar
Folder bar
Folder list
Outlook bar
Contacts
Info pane
Status bar

Headers pane
Preview pane header
Preview pane

◀

Starting Outlook Express

1 Start Outlook Express from the Start menu or its desktop icon.

2 Identify the marked areas. If you are working on a friend's PC, check before you read any messages! If it's your own PC, and the software has been installed recently, you should have a welcome message from Microsoft.

10

Starting Outlook Express (cont.)

The three key elements of the Outlook Express window are the Folder list, the Headers pane and the Preview pane. There are another six elements that can be included in the display. Apart from the Headers pane, every element is optional and can be easily switched off if you decide that you do not want it.

- The Headers pane is the only part of the display which is not optional, but even here you can control the layout and which items are displayed.
- The Folder list shows your email and news folders. New email folders can be created if needed, and newsgroup folders are created automatically when you subscribe to groups. The contents of the current folder are displayed in the Headers area.
- The Preview pane displays the current message from the Headers area. If this pane is turned off, messages are displayed in a new window. The pane can sit below or beside the Headers – below is usually more convenient.
- The Views bar lets you switch between displaying all messages and those you have not yet read. The options are also available on the View menu.
- The Folder bar shows the name of the current folder.
- The Outlook bar is an alternative to the Folder list for moving between folders. This is something of a hangover from Outlook (Express's big brother), which has a calendar, contacts book and other features that can be reached through the Outlook bar. In Outlook Express, this bar is a waste of screen space.
- The Preview pane header repeats the From and Subject details from the Headers area.
- The Contacts area shows the people in your Address Book. You can start a message to someone by double-clicking on their entry in this list. As there are other – equally convenient – ways to start new messages, you may want to reduce screen clutter by not displaying this list.

- The Info pane is occasionally used by Outlook Express to display information. Most people will find this a total waste of screen space.
- The Status bar, as always, helps to keep you informed of what's going on. Amongst other things, it tells you how many messages are in a folder, and shows the addresses behind hyperlinks in emails.

10

Exploring the toolbar ▶

Outlook Express has a lot of commands that most of us will rarely use, and if you don't join the newsgroups (see Chapter 10), there are some that you will never use at all. In practice, all the commands that you will use regularly can be found on buttons on the toolbar.

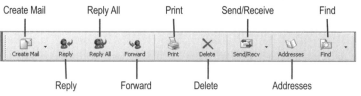

Create Mail

Click the button to start a new message in plain text or with the default formatting, or click the arrow to open a drop-down list.

Reply

Starts a new message to the sender of the current message – the same as Reply to Sender on the Message menu.

Reply All

Sends a reply to all the people who had copies of the message – the same as Message > Reply to All.

Forward

Copies the message into the New Message window, ready for you to send it on to another person, adding your own comments if you like. The same as Message > Forward.

Print

Prints the current message, using the default printer settings.

Delete

Deletion is a two-stage process. Clicking this button transfers the selected message(s) to the Deleted Items folder. Messages are then deleted from there when you close Outlook Express or when you delete them from the Deleted Items folder.

Send/Receive

Sends anything sitting in the Outbox and picks up any new mail. If there's something in your Outbox that you do not want to send yet, e.g. a message with a big attachment that will take a long time to send, open the Tools menu and use Receive All instead.

Similarly, if you are in a hurry to send a message but do not have time to deal with incoming mail, you can use Tools > Send All.

Addresses

Opens your Address Book, to add a new contact, or to manage existing ones.

Find

Will search through your stored messages, on the basis of the sender, subject, text within the message, date or other factors.

10

Reading an email message ▶

Unlike snail mail, email does not get delivered directly to you. Instead, it goes into a mailbox at the provider and you must go online to get it. You can set Outlook Express to check for new mail automatically on start-up and/or at regular intervals while you are online, or you can pick up your mail when you feel like it.

When messages arrive, they are dropped into the Inbox folder. Opening them for reading is very straightforward. After reading, you can reply if you like, and the message can be deleted or you move them to another folder – you might want to keep some for future reference. You can also just leave the message in the Inbox for the time being.

1 Start Outlook Express,

2 If you are not online already, get connected now.

3 Click the Send/Receive button drop-down arrow then select Receive All. Wait while the messages come in.

4 Select Inbox in the Folder list, if necessary.

5 Click anywhere on a message's line in the Header pane to open the message in the Preview pane. After reading the message...

6 If you don't want it any more, click ✕ .

7 If you want to leave it in the Inbox for the time being, click on the header line of the next message to read that.

8 If you want to respond to it, click 📧 .

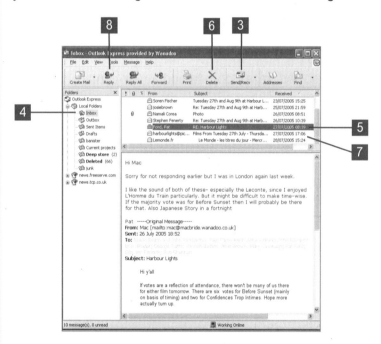

The Address Book isn't just a convenience, it is also an essential tool for email. Addresses are rarely easy to remember and if you get just one letter wrong, the message won't get through. But if an address is stored in your Address Book, you can pick it from there whenever you need it.

Addresses can be added to the Book in two ways: you can type them in directly, or if you are replying to people who have written to you, you can get Outlook Express to copy their addresses into the Book.

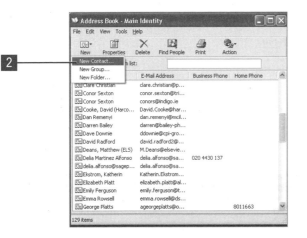

1 Click the [Add] button or open the Tools menu and select Address Book.

2 When the Address Book opens, click the New button and select New Contact.

3 Type in the person's name, splitting it into First, Middle and Last – the separate parts can be used for sorting the list. You can miss out any you don't need, or put the whole name into one slot.

4 Add a brief Nickname if you like – this can be used for selecting addresses later.

5 Type the address in the Email addresses slot, then click [Add].

10

Adding an address to the Address Book (cont.)

The Address Book can store more than just the email address. You can also add other contact information – home and business addresses and phone number, NetMeeting details – whatever is relevant; there is also space for the names of your contact's spouse and children, and even their birthday and anniversary dates. How much you put here is entirely up to you.

6 Switch to the Home or Business tab if you want to store the snail mail address or phone number.

7 Switch to the Personal tab if you want to add family details or dates to remember.

8 Click OK.

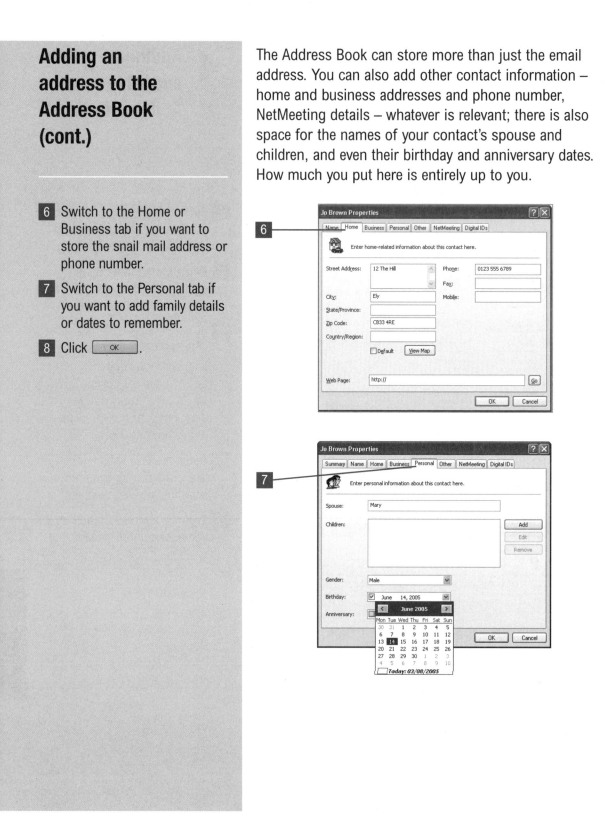

If there are only a couple of dozen entries in your Address Book, you should be able to find a contact simply by scrolling through the list. As the numbers rise, it can take longer to spot the entry you need. There are two ways to find a contact.

The simplest is to type in the first few letters of the name. The list will then scroll to the first matching entry. If that is not the one you want, then it is probably just below.

The second way uses the Find routine. This does a more thorough search and matches parts of names, not just the first letters.

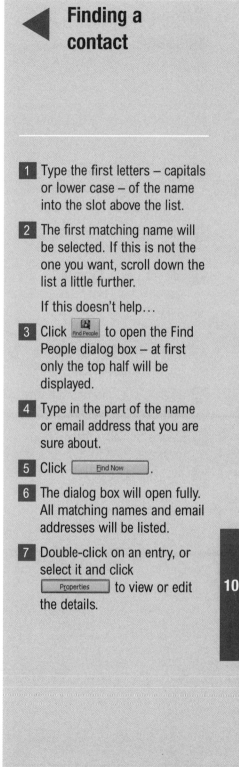

1 Type the first letters – capitals or lower case – of the name into the slot above the list.

2 The first matching name will be selected. If this is not the one you want, scroll down the list a little further.

If this doesn't help…

3 Click 🔍 Find People to open the Find People dialog box – at first only the top half will be displayed.

4 Type in the part of the name or email address that you are sure about.

5 Click Find Now.

6 The dialog box will open fully. All matching names and email addresses will be listed.

7 Double-click on an entry, or select it and click Properties to view or edit the details.

10

Writing a message

Messages are written in the New Message window. The main part of this is the writing area, but in the top part of the window there are several boxes which must be attended to.

- To: is the address of the recipient(s).
- Cc: (carbon copy) is for the addresses of those people, if any, to whom you want to send copies.
- You can also have Bcc: (blind carbon copy) recipients if you select their names from your Address Book. These people will not be listed, as the To and Cc recipients will be, at the top of the message.
- Subject: a few words outlining the nature of your message, so that your recipients know what's coming.

1 Open the File menu, point to New and select Mail Message or click 📭.

2 Click 📧 To: to open your Address Book.

3 Select a contact and click To: ->, Cc: -> or Bcc: ->, to copy the name into a recipient box.

Repeat Step 3 if you want to add more recipients.

4 Click OK to return to the New Message window.

5 Enter a Subject for the message.

6 Type the message.

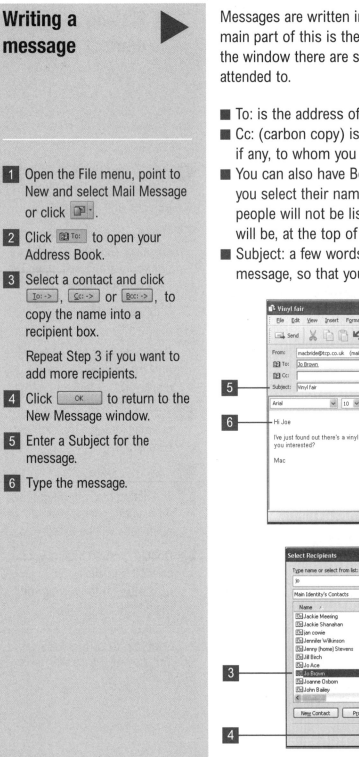

A message can be sent immediately after it has been written, or stored in the Outbox to be sent later. If you have a broadband connection, you would normally be online while you are writing the messages, and would send messages immediately. If you connect through the normal phone line, being online ties up the phone and (probably) costs money. In this case, you would be better to write your messages offline, store them in the Outbox then send all the new ones in one batch.

You can set the options so that either the Send button will send immediately or it will store messages. If you want to handle a message differently, there are Send and Send Later commands.

7 Click [Send] to use the default Send option.

or

8 Open the File menu and select Send Message or Send Later.

9 When you have finished all your writing, if there are messages in the Outbox, click [Send/Receive]. If you aren't online, the Connect dialog box will appear, ready to connect to your ISP.

Timesaver tip

If you forget to send the messages in the Outbox, Outlook Express will prompt you to send them before closing down. And if you close down without sending them, it will prompt you again next time that you start Outlook Express.

10

Replying to an email

Replying to someone else's email is the simplest and most reliable way to send a message, because the address is already there for you.

When you start to reply, the original text may be copied into your message. You can decide whether or not this should happen, and how the copied text is to be displayed – these controlled from the Tools > Options dialogue box. For the moment, go with the default settings.

1 When you click [Reply] the Compose window will open.

2 The To: field will already have the email address in it – though it may actually display the person's name. Don't worry about that.

3 The Subject: field will have the original Subject text, preceded by 'Re:'. Edit this if you like.

4 The message area may have the original text copied in. You can edit or delete this if you like.

5 Add you own message.

6 Click [Send].

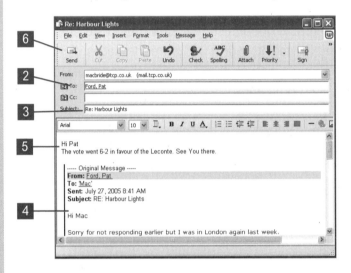

If someone sends you a message that you would like to share with other people, you can do this easily by forwarding. The subject and message are copied into the New Message window, so all you have to do is add the address of the recipients and any comments of your own.

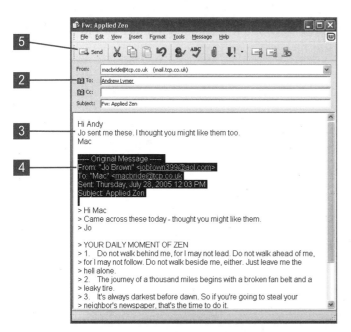

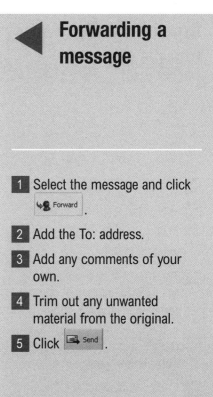

Forwarding a message

1. Select the message and click Forward.

2. Add the To: address.

3. Add any comments of your own.

4. Trim out any unwanted material from the original.

5. Click Send.

10

Attaching a file to a message ▶

Images, documents, music, programs and other non-text files can be sent by mail, attached to messages. As the mail system was designed for transmitting plain text, other files have to be converted to text for transfer, and back to binary on receipt. Outlook Express handles these conversions for you, but you need to be aware of the conversion, because it increases the size of file by about 50%. Big files get even bigger.

1 Start a new message as usual.

2 Open the Insert menu and select File Attachment... or click 📎 .

3 The Insert Attachment dialog box is essentially the same as the Open File dialog box. If you are looking for a picture, it may help if you switch to Thumbnails view.

4 Locate and select the file, then click Attach .

5 The file will be listed in a new Attach slot beneath the Subject line. Complete the message.

6 Click 📧 Send and wait – it takes a few moments for the system to convert the file.

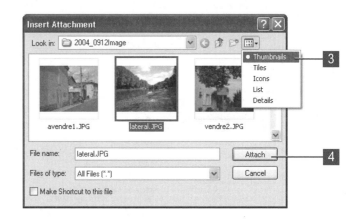

You'll know if an incoming message has an attachment as there will be a little paperclip icon beside it in the header list. If you have opted to show the preview pane header, you will also find a larger clip icon there.

For this next exercise you need a message with an attached file. So, you can either wait until someone sends you one, or you can attach a file to a message, set it to send later – so that it is in the Outbox – and then open the message. (And don't forget to delete it later if you only created the message to test the procedure!).

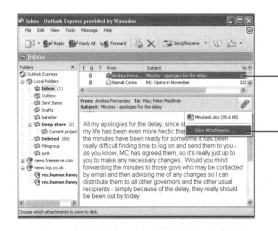

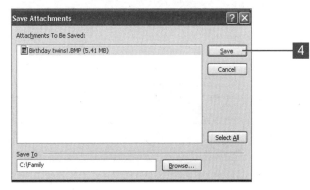

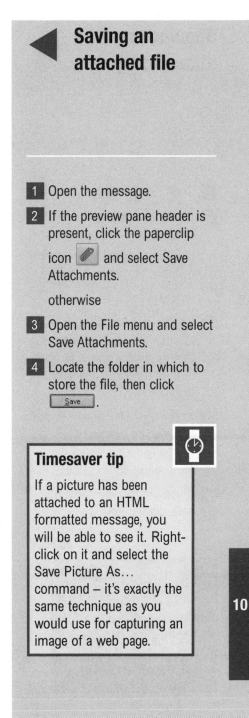

◀ Saving an attached file

1 Open the message.

2 If the preview pane header is present, click the paperclip icon 📎 and select Save Attachments.

otherwise

3 Open the File menu and select Save Attachments.

4 Locate the folder in which to store the file, then click Save .

Timesaver tip

If a picture has been attached to an HTML formatted message, you will be able to see it. Right-click on it and select the Save Picture As… command – it's exactly the same technique as you would use for capturing an image of a web page.

10

Opening an attachment

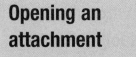

1. Open the message.

2. If the preview pane header is present, click the paperclip icon 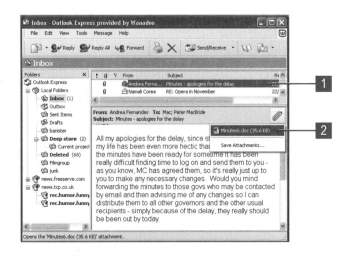 and select the name of the attachment.

   otherwise

3. Double-click on the message to open it in its own window, then righ-click on the filename in the Attach line and select Open.

4. At the Mail Attachment dialog box, think again and if you have any doubts about the file's safety, click Cancel.

5. If you are confident that it is safe, click Open.

Important !

Never open an executable file unless you have been expecting it and are absolutely certain that it is safe.

You can open an attachment directly from a message, without saving it. But take care. Some very nasty viruses are spread through email attachments. You get a message, apparently from an acquaintance, and when you open it, the virus program is executed. Typically, it will go through your address book, sending virus-laden messages to your contacts, and it may also destroy the files on the hard drive.

Any executable file (program) may be a virus. Common extensions for executable files include: .exe, .com, .bat, .vbx. Viruses can also be hidden in macros – programs that run within applications. These can be a problem in Word, Excel and PowerPoint. If you have any of these, make sure that they are set for high security in respect of macros. Go to the Tools menu, point to Macros, select Security… and set the level to High.

There are several ways in which you can customise your display. The first of these is to select the screen elements that you want to include in the layout. This is done in the Window Layout Properties dialog box. Simply tick or clear the ticks to turn elements on and off.

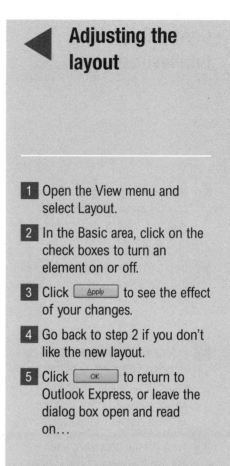

1 Open the View menu and select Layout.

2 In the Basic area, click on the check boxes to turn an element on or off.

3 Click [Apply] to see the effect of your changes.

4 Go back to step 2 if you don't like the new layout.

5 Click [OK] to return to Outlook Express, or leave the dialog box open and read on…

!

Important

The only elements that you really need ar the Folder List or the Outlook Bar – to move between your folders – and the Toolbar (unless you prefer to work from the menus).

10

Controlling the Preview pane

The Preview pane is optional – a message can also be opened into its own window. If the pane is present, it automatically displays whatever message is selected in the Headers pane. This can be useful, but it can also be a cause of problems – it all depends on how good the filters are at your internet service provider. If they are filtering out the spam and those messages that contain viruses, then the Preview pane can be used safely. If not, turn the pane off so that you control which messages are opened.

1 Open the View menu and select Layout... to open the Window Layout Properties dialog box.

2 In the Preview Pane area, click the checkbox to turn the pane on or off.

If the pane is on...

3 Select where the pane is to go – below is generally better as you can normally read the whole width of the message without scrolling the display.

4 Turn on the preview pane header if you want it – it simply repeats the From and Subject information from the Headers pane.

5 Click [OK].

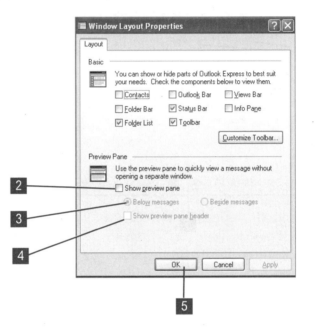

Jargon buster

Branch – in file management, the structure of sub-folders open off from a folder.

Browser – application specially designed for accessing and displaying the information in the World Wide Web. This is also true the other way: the web is an information system designed to be viewed on browsers.

Child folder – in file management, a sub-folder of a Parent.

Clipboard – windows has a special part of memory known as the Clipboard, which can be used for storing any kind of data – text, images, spreadsheets, complete files or small selected chunks. It can be used not just for copying or moving data within an application, but also between applications as the Clipboard can be accessed from any program.

Document – Windows uses 'document' to mean any file created by any application. A word-processed report is obviously a document, but so is a picture file from a graphics package, a data file from a spreadsheet, a video clip, sound file – in fact, any file produced by any program.

Driver – software that handles the interaction between the computer and a peripheral device. A printer driver converts the formatting information from an application into the right codes for the printer.

Email – electronic mail, a system for sending messages and files across networks.

Error-checking – the techniques used to make sure that data sent over the internet arrives intact. If a block of data is damaged, it is sent again.

Freeware – software ranging from well-meaning efforts of amateurs through to highly professional products like Acrobat Reader and Flash Player which are given away so that people can view the documents and files created by paid-for applications.

GUI – Graphical User Interface – the screen display for an operating system such as Windows, that uses images, icons and menus. Users start operations and make choices by clicking on these, rather than having to type in command words.

HTML – HyperText Markup Language, a system of instructions that browsers can interpret to display text and images. HTML allows hypertext links to be built into web pages.

ISP – Internet Service Provider – the company that supplies your connection to the internet.

Keyword – a keyword can be any word which might occur in the pages that you are looking for. If you give two or more, the system will only list pages which contain all those words.

Mail server – a computer that stores and handles email, either within a large organisation or at an ISP.

Net – short for internet – and internet is short for interlinked networks, which is what it is.

.Net passports – proof of identity that is accepted at many internet sites that use secure systems to protect confidential data – set one up from the User Accounts facility if you find that you need one.

Page – or web page, a document displayed on the web. It may be plain or formatted text; and may hold pictures, sounds and videos.

Parent folder – in file management, a folder that contains another.

Plain text – text without any layout or font formatting.

Root – in file management, the folder of the disk. All other folders branch off from the root.

Shareware program – one supplied on a try-before-you-buy basis. At the end of the trial period, you can continue to use the program for a small fee, typically £10 to £20. Shareware programs include the excellent WinZIP, file compression software, and Paint Shop Pro, a fully-equipped image editing and creation package.

Snail mail – the sort that is hand-delivered by the postman.

Template – document that has formatting and layout in place ready for your text. It may have some text and images in place already, e.g. headed paper for letters.

Web – the World Wide Web, also shortened to WWW or W3.

Troubleshooting guide